DATE DUE

DIABETES

**Recent Titles in the
Biographies of Disease Series**

Parkinson's Disease
Nutan Sharma

Depression
Blaise A. Aguirre

DIABETES

Andrew Galmer

LIBRARY

Biographies of Disease
Julie K. Silver, M.D., Series Editor

GREENWOOD PRESS
Westport, Connecticut • London

Library of Congress Cataloging-in-Publication Data

Galmer, Andrew.
  Diabetes / Andrew Galmer.
    p. cm. — (Biographies of disease, ISSN 1940-445X)
    Includes bibliographical references and index.
    ISBN 978-0-313-34257-8 (alk. paper)
    1. Diabetes—History. I. Title.
    RC660.G295 2008
    616.4′62—dc22   2008004526

British Library Cataloguing in Publication Data is available.

Library of Congress Catalog Card Number: 2008004526

ISBN: 978-0-313-34257-8
ISSN: 1940-445X

First published in 2008

Greenwood Press, 88 Post Road West, Westport, CT 06881
An imprint of Greenwood Publishing Group, Inc.
www.greenwood.com

Printed in the United States of America

♾™

The paper used in this book complies with the
Permanent Paper Standard issued by the National
Information Standards Organization (Z39.48–1984).

10 9 8 7 6 5 4 3 2 1

To my two wonderful nieces, Anya and Katya, whose thirst for knowledge and endless curiosity are a constant reminder to never stop questioning and never stop learning

Contents

Series Foreword

E very killer has a story to tell, and so it is with diseases as well: about how it started long ago and began to take the lives of its innocent victims, about the way it hurts us, and about how we are trying to stop it. In this *Biographies of Disease* series, the authors tell the stories of the diseases that we have come to know and fear.

The stories of these killers have all of the components that make for great literature. There is incredible drama played out in real-life scenes from the past, present, and future. You'll read about how men and women of science stumbled trying to save the lives of those they aimed to protect. Turn the pages and you'll also learn about the amazing success of those who fought the killer and won, saving thousands of lives in the process.

If you don't want to be a health professional or research scientist now, when you finish this book you may think differently. The men and women in this book are heroes who often risked their own lives to save ours. This is the biography of a killer, but it is also the story of real people who made incredible sacrifices to stop it in its tracks.

Julie K. Silver, M.D.
Assistant Professor, Harvard Medical School
Department of Physical Medicine and Rehabilitation

Preface

Diabetes is frequently taught in terms of signs and symptoms of pathology, often leaving out its greater effects on society, economics, and mankind. *Diabetes* is designed to provide a balanced account of diabetes in terms of disease processes and impacts across the globe historically and in the present day. The text follows a linear timeline of diabetes as first discussed in the ancient times and follows the course of the disease in a social and biological progression. It is written in a stepwise and logical manner allowing the reader to follow the "life" of diabetes from its infancy into maturity. This text is to be used by students and others to learn about diabetes in a unique way never before presented in a unified manner, with the intent to show the dramatic and powerful effects of this disease on various entities.

HOW TO USE THIS BOOK

Readers will receive information in a biographical timeline approach to diabetes that can be read in a sequential manner that layers information onto the foundation of the previous chapter. The depth of knowledge and the span of information included make this book a perfect addition to an institution's library or to a personal collection. Students along with others will benefit from a thorough but comprehendible analysis of the medical and social criteria of the disease. Each chapter covers its own dissertation of subject matter and can be read separately with a sense of completeness depending on the interests of the reader. Each chapter is divided into subchapters that contain relevant information on the topic at hand.

Chapter 1 begins with a historical discussion of ancient analysis of diabetes, including crude testing devices and treatments by scientists and physicians across the globe. We follow the disease with the maturation of science with advancements leading to a more complete understanding of the entity especially throughout the Renaissance and modern era. Chapter 2 recaps physiology of the human body that is pertinent to understanding diabetes, acting as a foundation for understanding normal functions that can go awry in diabetes. The objective is to learn the basic functions of cells and how they affect the intricate workings of organ systems within the body. Chapter 3 focuses on the various forms of diabetes in regards to mechanisms, clinical presentations, and complications. The reader will understand why the human body reacts in certain ways in relation to pathology. Chapter 4 explains how physicians test and treat diabetes, including diet therapies, lifestyle changes, and conventional pharmaceutical treatment that is standard in today's medicine. Chapter 5 is an analysis of how diabetes affects the individual, the United States, and global population in respect to socioeconomic factors. Statistical correlations regarding cost of healthcare, social discrepancy, and quality of life are mentioned in detail. The text concludes with current research that is being conducted in the field, including drug therapies, genetics, and new forms of insulin administration.

ACKNOWLEDGMENTS

I thank Julie Silver for granting me the opportunity to be part of such a momentous collaboration. Her numerous publications and help throughout the project were a great inspiration to me, giving me hope and strength along the way.

In addition, I thank my team of research assistants, Jessica Matosko, Libi Rind, Alex Paulenoff, and Nicolas Herman, who helped to accumulate a wide variety of information from numerous sources whose contributions made this textbook possible.

Introduction

The word "diabetes" is a powerful one. It is unlike any other word, unique in its own ways and known to many languages. This word elicits numerous emotions running the gamut of angst and hope, defining not only a disease but also a deep and profound history of medical science and affecting individuals in all parts of the world. The word diabetes stems from the ancient Greek word meaning "to siphon," describing a commonality shared by diabetics. Now it is a universal term that is used in hospitals, political meetings, and households symbolizing a powerful and widespread disease that has reached epidemic proportions. For individuals, diabetes can be a frightening realization of lifelong illness associated with morbid consequences.

For thousands of years, scientists have been struggling with the daunting task of understanding the complex workings of the disease, facing a constant battle with this entity. The first known historical mention of diabetes is seen in the Ebers Papyrus, which was written by the ancient Egyptians more than 3,500 years ago. The signs and symptoms were discussed in depth, which led to theories on treatment and prevention. Nations throughout time have been involved in a collaborative effort to understand diabetes through observation and experimentation with hopes of treating the disease. Examples of diagnosis included tasting the urine of diabetics along with using ants to analyze specimens. Although crude in their methodology, early scientists helped to prepare a foundation onto which future studies were conducted.

Despite the increased levels of the disease among the general public, the past hundred years have produced technological advancements and treatments that have been able to significantly decrease the many morbid complications associated with diabetes. Scientists such as Banting and Langerhans conducted laboratory research that led to a better understanding of the disease. This era led to the development of insulin, oral medications, and blood monitoring devices that changed the outlook on the diabetic condition forever.

The current world acknowledges diabetes as an epidemic that must be addressed with the utmost importance. There are sixteen million people living with diabetes in the United States currently, and 200,000 people die annually from the disease and its complications. Although there is no cure for diabetes, it is possible to control the disease through medication, diet, and exercise. These methods help bring the abnormal sugar levels in the body to a normal bodily state to preserve the internal balance of the physiological system (National Institute of Diabetes 2005).

Diabetes is a serious lifelong medical condition dealing with abnormal control of sugars in the bloodstream that causes a variety of symptoms and serious associated complications. It is medically described as a collection of metabolic disorders that result in chronically elevated blood glucose levels. Both type 1 and type 2 diabetics are unfortunately prone to the morbid complications associated with hyperglycemia, leading to amputations, cardiac failure, eye problems, and kidney failure. However, with proper control of sugar levels, prevention is possible. Today, individuals can monitor blood sugars with portable meters and take medications to help control their condition. Frequent visits to physicians and prevention of complications are the standard of care.

As a medical student rotating through many fields of medicine, I encountered diabetics on a daily basis. Some of these patients are newly diagnosed, whereas others have been fighting the disease for decades. Treating these patients was on a highly individualized basis, considering the length and severity of disease. During clerkships, I noticed the manner in which diabetes presents itself and the way those who suffer with it daily live out their lives in struggle, adding another dimension to treatment. The face of diabetes manifests itself not on the cellular level but, tragically, as an increasingly common global epidemic as well. Apart from the small percentage of diabetics who are genetically prone to the disease, seemingly benign activities such as poor diet and low activity levels put millions of others at risk as well. The global community has responded to this epidemic by investing ample amounts of money and resources into treatment and prevention, but the intended outcomes have not been met and public susceptibility is on the rise.

1

The Birth of Diabetes

Mankind has been struggling with diabetes for thousands of years. Its consequences have been documented and discussed by physicians and medicine men spanning numerous eras and civilizations. The history of diabetes began long before the establishment of its popularized name. In ancient texts, it is described by the effects it has on the body. Ancient techniques for diagnosing and treating diabetes laid the groundwork for medical developments that have contributed to improving the quality of life for diabetic patients. What began as a series of common signs and symptoms recognized by ancient healers has become a modern science and a topic of active investigation and research in today's medical field. A careful study of the life story of diabetes will reveal different approaches to both diagnosis and treatment. The contributions of many cultures will be explored. A disease of such significance warrants discussion of its effects on mankind throughout human history.

The current world acknowledges diabetes as an epidemic that must be addressed with the utmost importance. There are sixteen million people living with diabetes in the United States currently, and 200,000 people die annually from the disease and its complications. Although there is no cure for diabetes, it is possible to control the disease through medication, diet, and exercise.

These methods help bring the abnormal sugar levels in the body to a normal bodily state to preserve the internal balance of the physiological system (National Institute of Diabetes 2005).

To better understand the intricacies of diabetes, it is necessary to begin with the fundamental principles. Diabetes is a term used to describe the imbalance of sugars caused by a defective or ineffective production of insulin. This causes inefficient glucose utilization. Because the glucose is not transported into the cell, it stays in the bloodstream and causes a condition called hyperglycemia, or elevated levels of sugar in the blood. Diabetes mellitus is literally translated as "to pass through sweetened with honey," referring to urine as being sweetened with the excess sugars of the diabetic. The kidneys react to the excess glucose by filtering it out of the circulatory system to be frequently excreted in urine, thus giving diabetes its name. The physiology of diabetes leads to symptoms of hyperglycemia, frequent urination, excessive thirst, sensation of numbness, nephropathy, or worsening kidney function, retinopathy leading to eventual vision loss, and many other ill effects (Wilmore 2004).

The subject of diabetes must not be described solely in terms of the biological and pathological effects, but rather in conjunction with key historical contributions that help construct the modern understanding of the disease. Diabetes has caught the interest of many physicians throughout human history and has been discussed in numerous texts ranging from the Ebers Papyrus in Egypt to today's *New York Times*. These artifacts show how different cultures cope with a single disease using a wide variety of approaches. Before the discovery of insulin and sulfonylurea drugs, the ancient cultures of Egypt, Rome, India, and China dealt with the effects of diabetes in their own unique ways. With the advent of sea travel and the implementation of trade routes, their ideas spread across the globe, effectively unifying the medical community. The importance of this unification had a great effect on today's perception of the diabetic condition.

In this chapter, we will discuss the historical course of diabetes from ancient civilizations through the Middle Ages. This historical epoch will tell the story of how diabetes appeared in written texts for the first time and won the attention of numerous physicians in cultures throughout the world. We will see similar trends about the disease that were found throughout the globe and how different techniques were used to analyze them. The historical evidence that is available on diabetes is fundamental to a complete understanding of its impact on the modern era and demonstrates mankind's incessant struggle with this disease.

From using ants for analyzing urine to portable electronic blood monitors, the science of diabetes and its impact on human health has changed drastically. Although the signs and symptoms have remained the same, the means of treatment and care have become fundamentally more developed over time. We will follow the contributions of physicians throughout history, along with advances in scientific techniques and principles, beginning with the earliest known recorded evidence of diabetes in ancient Egypt and ending with contributions from major physicians of the Middle Ages whose work can be recognized in the modern world of diabetes.

ANCIENT EGYPTIANS: DOCUMENTING MEDICAL HISTORY

By today's standards, early medicine used crude, yet accessible, techniques for assessing an individual's ailment and linking it to a disease. Ancient Egyptians were the earliest of civilizations to document and record such medical findings. Displaying limited, but advanced, knowledge of medicine, Egyptian physicians used these remedies for treating various illnesses and diseases. Contributions from the Egyptians led to the creation of a medical document dating back to 1552 BC, the Ebers Papyrus, which contains a collection of 700 remedies for a wide array of medical obstacles ranging from dog bites to skull fractures (see Figure 1.1). The Ebers Papyrus, written in hieratic script, is the oldest and most complete medical record from ancient Egypt (Kavic 1997). There is substantial evidence showing that the Ebers Papyrus was copied from numerous books many centuries older, dating as far back as 3400 BC. Hesy-Ra, a well respected ancient Egyptian physician, made major contributions to the Ebers Papyrus. It is in this document that we find the first known documentation of diabetes (Scheiner 2004). Of the 110-page scroll, there is only one mention of a common sign of diabetes: polyuria, or frequent urination. It is important to note that there is some controversy on this finding because many other pathological conditions can cause polyuria, such as chronic renal disease, hypocalcaemia, and hypokalemia (Powers 1996). Nonetheless, this reference is important because individuals with diabetes commonly exhibit signs of high blood glucose, frequent urination, and excessive thirst.

Accompanying this reference are various methods of treatment. For instance, a "measuring glass filled with elderberry, fibers of the asit plant, fresh milk, beer-swill, flower of the cucumber, dates and water from the bird pond" were all suggested to be taken to reinstate a normal urinary process (Sanders 2001). Another suggested method to prevent urinary ailments was to take enemas of "olive oil, honey, sweet beer, sea salt, and seeds of the wonder fruit" (Sanders 2001). These seemingly odd techniques are only a few of many that were used by the ancient Egyptians in treating illness, which influenced neighboring countries to continue with similar traditions.

Figure 1.1. Ebers Papyrus. Written in 1550 BC, this papyrus from ancient Egypt is one of oldest known medical documents and contains the first written description of the diabetic condition. *Courtesy of The National Library of Medicine.*

The tradition of Egyptian medicine continued years after the Ebers Papyrus was composed. During the third century BC, an Egyptian writer, Apollonius Memphites, authored a work titled *On The Names of the Parts of the Human Body*. He described the abundance of urine that is excreted by diabetes as a bodily state "without retention." This description is similar to that of the Ebers Papyrus, which was written 1,000 years earlier (Markwick 1842). Apollonius took the description one step further by describing the urinary condition as if it was "without delay." In other words, he noticed urination shortly after the intake of fluids in diabetics (Swartout-Corbeil 2002).

Demetrios of Apameia later described this by the word we know today: diabetes. In 200 BC, diabetes was used to describe this disease process. Demetrios noticed common trends in diabetics and grouped them together to form a more unified definition of the disease (Papaspyros 1989). In other parts of the world, people noticed similar signs and performed more specific tests to help better diagnose such individuals.

ANTS AND URINE

In India, Ayurvedic medicine took notice of diabetes as shown by Sanskrit texts, which date back to 400 BC. Before the creation of these ancient Indian manuscripts, Ayurvedic medicine had been preserved by oral tradition that originated within small Hindu tribes. Practitioners highly valued the harmony of physical, mental, social, and spiritual worlds, which explains the literal meaning of Ayurvedic as "the science of life." The oral tradition was eventually replaced by the creation of various manuscripts. Indian healers edited these manuscripts, each contributing to what became a unified pool of knowledge (Dick 1998). Two of the most influential texts include *Shushruta Samhita* and *Charaka Samhita*, both of which make references to diabetes.

In *Shushruta Samhita*, we find the concept of "madhu-meh," or sweet urine. This finding is greatly significant and is the first known mention of the nature of a diabetic's urine. Remarkably, it was 2,400 years ago that Indians described the particulars of diabetes used in modern day medicine as a diagnostic feature (Samhita 1949). Although their diagnostic equipment was scanty, their resourcefulness allowed them to devise a method for checking urinary glucose levels. Indian healers would instruct suspected diabetics to urinate near an anthill. If the ant colony began to congregate near the urine sample, it would suggest a positive finding. The use of ants helped to quickly and accurately diagnose an individual with diabetes. This example and others like it demonstrate the ingenuity of the ancient Indians.

Shushruta Samhita was later modified by the Indian healer Charaka and became known as *Charaka Samhita*. People who follow alternative forms of medicine reference *Charaka Samhita*, even today. Charaka added his own findings on diabetes and explained the disease by describing two different types of diabetes known today to be type 1 (insulin dependant) and type 2 (non-insulin dependent; Goldberg 2002). Although he did not have access to electronic blood monitors or genetic sequencers, he was able to discern the two types by noting similarities in urine consistencies of two groups: thin, young individuals and obese elderly (Tillotson 2001).

ANCIENT GREEKS

Whereas the ancient Indians were using ants to test for urine consistency, ancient Greek medicine was being transformed by heavy influence from

Figure 1.2. Hippocrates, also known as the father of medicine, is famous for being the first physician to reject supernatural causes of disease. *Courtesy of The National Library of Medicine.*

Hippocrates, considered to be the father of medicine (see Figure 1.2). Among other things, he studied art, philosophy, and medicine. Hippocrates' works changed the way medicine was practiced by physicians, and modern day doctors follow his ideology. Furthermore, he dismantled the wall between science and human nature that can be seen in the modern version of the Hippocratic Oath: "I will remember that there is art to medicine as well as science, and that warmth, sympathy, and understanding may outweigh the surgeon's knife or the chemist's drug" (Edelstein 1943). His contributions to medicine can be noted in *The Hippocratic Corpus*, a compilation of his works dating back to the third century BC. At the time, Hippocrates uniquely dismissed all spiritual and supernatural causes of disease. Through elimination of the divine, he was able to make diagnoses based solely on observations and physical findings. Although Hippocrates made very little reference to diabetes, his clinical proficiency and knowledge of nephrology enabled him to make clinical observations related to diabetes.

The ancient Greek physician and student of Hippocrates, Aretaeus of Cappadocia, wrote numerous works on the study of diseases during the second century. He was considered one of the most influential physicians of his time and contributed a vast bank of knowledge to Greek civilization (Walford 2000). In one of his texts, he uses the term diabetes to describe the most common sign of this disease, polyuria. Based on his observations, he noticed that diabetic individuals urinate soon after drinking. His text included a more detailed account of diabetes than any other medical text before it. In it, he said, "Diabetes is a dreadful affliction, not very frequent among men, being a melting down of the flesh and limbs into urine. The patients never stop making water and the flow is incessant, like the opening of the aqueducts. Life is short, unpleasant and painful, thirst unquenchable, drinking excessive and disproportionate to the large quantity of urine, for yet more urine is passed . . . if for a while they abstain from drinking, their mouths become parched and their bodies dry; the viscera seem scorched up, the patients are affected by nausea, restlessness and a burning thirst, and within a short time they expire" (Poretsky 2002). In addition to this description of diabetes, Aretaeus discussed a need for a cure for this disease. This remedy remains unclear in his writings, yet he attempted to demonstrate that insatiable thirst is a chronic condition among diabetics.

During the same time Aretaeus was practicing medicine, Claudius Galen, the son of a wealthy architect, was able to pursue a well-rounded spectrum of medical interests. He was fascinated by the art of medicine and attended prestigious medical schools abroad. He began his career in Pergamum, studying clinical cases with the utmost scrutiny and thoroughness. With such impressive experience, Galen documented his medical knowledge in seventeen volumes, titled *On the Localisation of Diseases*. In it, he spoke of diabetes in terms of symptoms and organ failure (Luderitz 2002). He described the dehydrated status of the individual and placed blame on the kidneys. Galen wrote, "I am of the opinion that the kidneys too are affected in the rare disease which some people call diabetes. For my own part I have seen the disease till now only twice when the patients suffered from an inextinguishable thirst" (Henschen 1969). Although his clinical experience with diabetes was limited, his stance on the pathophysiology is noteworthy. He wrongly assumed that the problem lied in kidney function. Nonetheless, his method of practice and commitment to a thorough study of disease became a benchmark for medicine, influencing early European and Islamic practices.

BALANCED MEDICINE

Early Chinese medicine focuses on energy and balance. The concept of yin-yang and the importance of the five phases (wood, fire, earth, metal, and water) are fundamental to healers. Chinese medicine describes the yin and the yang as forces that must be in balance to ensure good health. Imbalances are corrected through the use of acupuncture, herbal remedies, exercise, diet, and lifestyle, thereby reestablishing the health of the individual. This ideology is stressed in the *Nan-Ching* document from the second century AD. This doctrine is considered a monumental literary work in Chinese medicine that couples sinister pathologies with unbalanced energy forces (Unschuld 1986). In effect, diabetes was mentioned in this text only by the common symptoms of thirst and polyuria. The symptoms are considered a result of poor energy balance, yet the sweet characteristic of the urine was not mentioned for several hundred years after the creation of the document.

The most prominent ancient Chinese physician, Chang Chung-Ching, lived during the creation of *Nan-Ching*. His contributions to medicine are well noted in his work *Treatise on Colds and Fevers*, which the Chinese deem to be the most influential medical book, second only to *Nan-Ching* (National Library of Medicine 2000). He offered Chinese medicine a more in-depth description of diabetes, which included "clouding of the urine, frigidity, and swelling of the lower limbs" (Medvei 1993). It is not uncommon for diabetics to experience these described symptoms, all common symptoms experienced by diabetics. Despite these insights, it would be another 300 years before any new treatment would be available.

ARABIC MEDICINE

Like the Chinese, the Islamic world during the Middle Ages experienced a boom in scientific and philosophical endeavors. It was a time of enlightenment and a search for wisdom. A major character in these advances is Rhazes, an Islamic physician who practiced in Persia during the ninth century AD. He developed new techniques in clinical medicine that led to a bettering of the practice. Rhazes spent much of his life studying clinical procedures and medical texts from neighboring countries. He compiled a twenty-volume book, *The Comprehensive Book on Medicine*, which incorporated a lifetime of clinical findings with insight on his medical research. It is in this text that we find mention of the symptoms of diabetes along with a suggested course of therapy. Rhazes suggested changes in nutritional regimens for treating various ailments, such as polyuria, rather than a strictly pharmacological management (Medvei 1993).

Avicenna was another Islamic physician held in high regard for his contributions to both Arabic and Western European medicine. Avicenna used philosophy to help him in thoroughly understanding medicine, because his religion prevented him from studying the internal workings of a human via dissection. With the arrival of the tenth century came Avicenna's major literary work the *Canon of Medicine*. This fourteen-volume text organized and explained disease processes along with recommendations for treatment. The *Canon of Medicine* was such a monumental contribution to medicine that medical facilities in Europe followed its practices for the next 600 years (Majeed 2005).

It is within the *Canon of Medicine* that we find detailed descriptions of diabetic symptoms along with a list of differential diagnoses. He distinguished between primary and secondary diabetes along with a description of the sugary consistency of urine. Also noted were problems with appetite, along with excessive thirst, decreased sexual function, and boils of the skin. He dedicated entire chapters to symptoms such as thirst, polyuria, and obesity. Unique to previous texts is his description of diabetic gangrene that is commonly found on the extremities of diabetic individuals (Prioreschi 2001). He also suggested a new method of treatment for the sweet urine, consisting of lupine, fenugreek, and zedoary seed. This combination of ingredients has proven to be helpful, even in modern medicine, for aiding in the reduction of glucose levels in the urine. Furthermore, Avicenna provides treatment methods for hypoglycemic coma and appetite dysfunctions, which can be useful for diabetics. Beyond diagnosis and treatment, Avicenna theorizes liver dysfunction to be the cause of diabetes, which is later rebuked by modern medicine (Reece, Coustan, and Gabbe 2004).

The twelfth century introduced Moses Maimonides, a physician well educated in rabbinical theory. He studied the medicine of ancient times with a large focus on the works of Galen. Maimonides is well known for his literary work *Fusul Musa*, which contained medical aphorisms on numerous subjects. In his work, he restated Galen's observations, as well as his belief that diabetes is caused by a failure of the kidneys and the bladder. He said, "I, too, have not seen it [diabetes] in the West, nor did any of my teachers under whom I studied mention that they had seen it. However, here in Egypt, in the course of approximately ten years, I have seen more than twenty people who suffered from this illness" (Rosner 1997). This shows that, from a clinical perspective, he believed that there was a direct correlation between warm climates and the incidence of diabetes.

During its early stages in history, diabetes was considered a vague and peculiar disease. Through careful analysis of ancient medical artifacts, we can look back to the beginnings of diabetes and follow its path across the globe. We explored textual references from cultures in Egypt, India, Greece, China, and Arabic lands. Egypt gave us the wonderful gift of a detailed collection of medical thought with the Ebers papyrus. Ayurvedic medicine from early Indian tribes told of creative techniques for diagnosing diabetes using ants. The ancient Greeks had numerous physicians that contributed to the diabetic description, including Hippocrates, Aretaeus, and Galen. The Chinese analyzed medicine through a lens of energies and balances, offering methods of treatment that preached abstinence from sex and alcohol. As time passed, physicians such as Rhazes, Avicenna, and Maimonides gave detailed descriptions of diabetes and connected the disease to specific organ systems. As time progressed, so did medical knowledge. This progress has been demonstrated by improvements in the descriptive language along with new and more effective treatments.

We have discussed the birth of diabetes in medicine, its early stages, and will continue to follow its development into the modern era. As the Middle Ages came to an end, medicine was faced with the challenge of expanding its explanations of diabetes and a proper treatment regimen. Meanwhile, physicians of the Renaissance were left with the daunting task of deciphering the unsolved mysteries of this disease. In the next chapter, we will discuss the development of diabetes in contributing countries during the Renaissance.

THE REBIRTH OF SCIENCE

The Renaissance in Europe brought a great change to the advancement of the medical field. Like art and philosophy, people began looking for new advancements in the world of medicine. Between the twelfth and seventeenth centuries, students of medicine began to question ancient medical studies of anatomy, instead looking for other causes and remedies of familiar ailments.

One early renaissance pioneer of medicine was a man named Theophrastus Bombastus von Honenheim, more commonly referred to as Paracelsus. Like others who sought enlightenment in Europe, Paracelsus believed that there was a link between medicine and the study of alchemy. In essence, Paracelsus was a pioneer in chemical medicine. He believed that the body acted as a laboratory for chemical reactions. With this belief, he surmised that disease was an imbalance of the chemicals within the body. Using his knowledge of alchemy, he would come up with various treatments using chemicals that could rebalance such deficiencies in the body. In the spirit of the Renaissance age, Paracelsus developed a rough foundation for what we now refer to as the scientific method. Through careful research, he hypothesized that the human body was composed of three basic substances: sulfur, mercury, and salt (Sanders 2001b). With this basic theory, he devised experiments to test his hypothesis, hoping to lead to the treatment of disease: "When he evaporated a liter of urine, he recovered 4 ounces of what he thought was salt—although it was actually sugar" (Sanders 2001b). Despite being incorrect, Paracelsus then concluded that the salt, which built up in the body, had an effect on the kidneys.

Adding on to this theory, he concluded that, when the kidneys could not overcome the impact of the salt through urine secretion, the overabundance of salt went on to affect other areas of the body.

Although Paracelsus was incorrect, he became the precursor for further diabetes research. Paracelsus found that "instead of uroscopy by ocular inspection, he proposed diagnosis by chemical analysis, distillation, and coagulation tests" (Magner 2005, 224). This method of diagnosis was a significant shift from the Galenic methods used during the Dark Ages and caused a rift in the medical community. At one point, it was recorded that "... in the middle of the St John's Day celebrations, Paracelsus led a band of cheering students into the market place. Here he triumphantly burned the works of Galen and Avicenna (just as Luther had publicly burned the missive from the Pope threatening him with excommunication)" (Strathern 2005, 81). Many saw Paracelsus' movement, heavily influenced by Luther, as a significant break from the Medieval and Arabic past.

The next significant figure in diabetes research is Thomas Willis. Willis, an English physician in the seventeenth century, rediscovered the sweet quality of urine in people suffering from diabetes. Although ancient medicine men had discovered this fact centuries before, it had been largely overlooked until Willis reintroduced his findings. More so, Willis "claimed that diabetes was primarily a disease of the blood and not the kidneys. Willis believed that the sweetness appeared first in the blood and was later found in the urine" (Sanders 2001b, 25). This theory is expanded on in the next century by an Englishman named Matthew Dobson. Furthering the use of the scientific method, Dobson did a series of experiments to prove that diabetes was, in fact, a disease affecting the bloodstream. First testing urine for sugary matter, Dobson then tested the blood of a diabetic, noting that, "the serum was sweetish, but ... not as sweet as the urine. It appears that the saccharine matter (found in the urine) was not formed in the secretory organ (the kidneys), but previously existed in the serum of the blood" (Sanders 2001b, 26). It is around this time that the term "diabetes mellitus" is coined by William Cullen. Mellitus is the Latin word for "honey," which is representative of the sweet taste of the urine found in diabetics. This adjective was added to the name to differentiate diabetes mellitus from another condition known as diabetes insipidus, a disorder resulting from the absence of an antidiuretic hormone in the brain. The diseases share common symptoms but, besides the name, have no common causes. In his 1769 work *Synopsis Nosologiae Methodicae*, Cullen notes these classifications, citing "a distinction between diabetes (mellitus), with urine of "the smell, colour and flavour of honey," and diabetes (insipidus) "with limpid but not sweet urine" (Sanders 2001b, 27). For the purposes of this book, the term diabetes will refer solely to diabetes mellitus.

The final major pioneer of diabetes research in the eighteenth century is the English physician John Rollo. Rollo is responsible for the first nutritional approach to diabetes control. His findings shifted research focus from the kidneys to the stomach. One of Rollo's experiments involved the recording of a man's diet and the resulting amounts of sugar found in his urine depending on what was ingested. After a thorough analysis of his findings, Rollo concluded that "'vegetable' matter—breads, grains, and fruits—increased the amount of sugar in the urine. 'Animal' matter—meat and fat—decreased the amount of sugar" (Sanders 2001b, 29). Because Rollo believed that diabetes was a disease of the stomach, he proposed that a controlled diet would be effective in limiting the stomach's production of sugar. Once again, these findings take mankind one step closer to the understanding of diabetes and the development of its treatment options.

In the nineteenth century, a French physiologist by the name of Claude Bernard made the next big step in diabetes research (see Figure 1.3). He found that sugar is formed in the liver and stored as glycogen. In a lecture he gave at the Collège de France in 1855, Bernard "indicated that the liver had two

Figure 1.3. Claude Bernard was a pioneer in the development of the scientific method still used today as a methodical and stepwise approach to experimentation. *Courtesy of The National Library of Medicine.*

secretions, and external secretion of bile and an internal secretion of sugar that passed directly into the blood" (Sanders 2001b, 31, 32). Furthermore, he made the link between this glucose present in the liver and the sugar found in the urine of diabetics. "Bernard was convinced that many of the vital functions which took place within the human body were highly complex. These could not be explained simply by observing its outer performance for this would be 'like trying to tell what is taking place inside a house by watching what enters through the door and what leaves by the chimney'" (Strathern 2005, 216). In Bernard's statement, one can see the use of Paracelsus' research methods. The advances in science allow Bernard to move beyond the simple observance of the body and begin the exploration of the body's inner workings. The relationship between the glycogen found in the liver and the sugar found in urine is reminiscent of the alchemic theories that Paracelsus preached, a complex mechanization of bodily function.

With this, we enter the twentieth century. Now we will shift our focus from history to some basic biology. To understand and appreciate the work these people have accomplished, it is imperative to have a general understanding of the body and how it contributes to the cause and cure for diabetes.

WHAT IS THE LIVER?

As with any disease, researchers push to find a cure; in doing so, these people must determine where and how the disease begins. For a long time, in the world of diabetes research, it was unclear what role the liver played. Furthermore, it became the job of researchers to determine how each organ functioned, to apply that knowledge to the application of treatment.

To begin, the liver is an organ that sits in the upper right quadrant of the abdomen. Its main function is to control the body's metabolic regularity. More specifically, the liver is responsible for a number of bodily functions, including the processing of amino acids, carbohydrates, lipids, and vitamins. It is also responsible for the removal of toxins and waste that build up in the body's blood flow. Within the context of the formation of diabetes, the liver plays a key role as the producer of blood sugar. If you recall Claude Bernard from the first section, he is said to have surmised that "it is the liver, transforming material assimilated in digestion, that dumps sugar into the blood stream" (Bliss 1982, 25). From this conjecture, Bernard proposed that diabetes was, perhaps, a disease of the liver. At the time, this theory made sense considering that the liver produced sugar in the body, and diabetes resulted with an overabundance of sugar in a patient's urine. Although he was not completely off on his theory, Bernard was still a long way from fully understanding diabetes.

Although the liver is not the most spotlighted organ, it is important to understand how it works in relation to the pancreas. Although the pancreas is the main organ associated with diabetes, it is the balance between the organs and regular bodily function that determines one's health.

WHAT IS THE PANCREAS?

The pancreas plays a vital role in the understanding of diabetes. It is the organ responsible for the production and secretion of insulin into the bloodstream. To get a better understanding of the pancreatic function, we will first examine the makeup of the pancreas.

To help you get an image of this pivotal organ, "the pancreas is a jelly-like gland, attached to the back of the abdomen behind and below the stomach. It is long and narrow and thin, irregular in size, but in humans usually measuring about $20 \times 6 \times 1$ centimeters and weighing about 95 grams" (Bliss 1982, 25). Furthermore, "the pancreas contains not one, but two systems of cells. There are the acini, or clusters of cells, which secrete the normal pancreatic juice. But scattered through the organ and penetrating the acini in such a way that they often seem to be floating in a sea of acinar cells, Langerhans found other cells, apparently unconnected to the acini" (Bliss 1982, 25). These cells, which we now call the islets of Langerhans, are the endocrine cells of the pancreas. These clusters "compose 1% to 2% of the pancreatic mass.... The islets of Langerhans contain four cell types, and each cell secretes a different hormone or peptide. The β cells compose 65% of the islet and secrete insulin. The α cells compose 20% of the islet and secrete glucagon" (Costanzo 2006, 420). For the purposes of this book, we will focus on the beta and alpha cells.

To get an idea of how the pancreas works, we can start with the fact that blood circulates insulin from the pancreas around the body. In return, insulin opens up cells in the body so glucose can enter them. Once glucose enters a cell, one of three things can happen. The first option is immediate use by the cell to create energy. The second option is cell storage of glucose in the form of glycogen for easy use at a later time. The final option is the conversion of glucose to fat, which can be stored long term and used at a later time.

Once the glucose in the bloodstream enters the various cells around the body, the blood glucose levels drop. It is the job of the pancreas to sense this drop and stop the production of insulin. If the pancreas fails to halt insulin production, the result is a condition called hypoglycemia. This means that there is too much sugar in the body. The overabundance of sugar is then discarded by various means of disposal, one of these being an overabundance of sugar in the diabetic's urine.

Now that you have a basic understanding of the body and its role in the formation of diabetes, we can explore the ways in which people discovered these roles. The next section will also discuss early treatments for diabetics.

ANIMAL RESEARCH AND FINDINGS

When people are not able to test medicine on other people, animals become an important part of the research process. Although is it a controversial subject matter today, animal testing has been a major part of medical advancement. Several of the major contributors to diabetes research have turned to animal experimentation to test theories and treatments for the disease. Whether or not one accepts testing of animals for medical purposes, it is a fact that, without these tests, the medical community would not have the same understanding of diabetes that it has today.

Claude Bernard, whom we discussed earlier in this chapter, is one of the first people to use animal testing in diabetes research. In an experiment to "determine the role of the pancreas in producing sugar in the urine (glycosuria)," Bernard "tied off the pancreatic ducts of dogs or blocked the ducts with injections of melted fats that solidified at body temperature" (Sanders 2001b, 32). Unfortunately Bernard's experiments were unsuccessful in producing the results he intended. The dogs' pancreases degenerated and they experienced abnormalities in digestion, yet the experiments did not yield the appearance of sugar in the dogs' urine. Although this seems like an experiment performed in vain, it is not the case. This only proved that the pancreas produces some secretion that come from ducts and other secretions that go directly into the bloodstream.

In another experiment Bernard "demonstrated links between the central nervous system and diabetes when he observed temporary hyperglycaemia (*piqûre* diabetes) when the medulla of conscious rabbits was transfixed with a needle" (Williams and Pickup 2004, 7). Although this seems like an extreme measure in the study of diabetes, many people came to understand the necessity of such work. Bernard often faced fierce criticism from denouncers of vivisection (the practice of dissecting or cutting into living animals) but was later backed by none other than Charles Darwin. Darwin, who had previously shunned the practice, stated, "Physiology cannot possibly progress except by means of experiments on living animals, and I feel the deepest conviction that he who retards the progress of physiology commits a crime against mankind" (Strathern 2005, 226). It is this sentiment, which resonates across countless ethical issues in the name of medicine, that people continue to debate today.

Claude Bernard was not the only person to explore science and medicine through animal experimentation. It was Paul Langerhans' experiments on rabbits that allowed scientists to begin to understand the makeup and functions of the pancreas. In his quest to explore the physiology of the pancreas, Langerhans "using a primitive light microscope ... injected the pancreatic ducts of rabbits with Berlin-blue dye, described the pancreatic duct system, and traced the ducts to the acinar glandular cells, which secrete digestive enzymes" (Sanders 2001b, 33). A second set of cells scattered around the pancreatic tissue did not seem to "communicate directly with the excretory ducts," and Langerhans described them as "small cells of almost perfect homogenous content and of polygonal form, with round nuclei without nucleoli, mostly lying together in pairs or small groups" (Sanders 2001b, 33). Despite admitting that he did not understand the function of these cells, they were eventually named "islets of Langerhans" in honor of their discoverer. It was eventually discovered that "type 1 diabetes is due to destruction of B-cells in the pancreatic islets of Langerhans with resulting loss of insulin production" (Watkins 2003, 2).

Another set of animal researchers in the world of diabetes are Oskar Minkowski and Joseph von Mering. In 1889, the two men removed the pancreas from a dog to see whether it was "essential for life" (Williams and Pickup 2004, 8). On removal of the pancreas, the dog showed several common symptoms associated with glycosuria and hyperglycaemia, including thirst, polyuria, and wasting. The experiment proved that "a pancreatic disorder caused diabetes, but they did not follow up on the observation," which put a slight halt on the progression of diabetes research.

Thirty-two years after Minkowski and von Mering unarguably link pancreatic function to diabetes, using dogs, two more men make a historically invaluable discovery with canine research. In 1921, at the University of Toronto, Frederick Banting and his assistant Charles Best successfully isolate insulin from dog pancreases. To do so, they "made chilled extracts of dog pancreas, injected them into pancreactectomized diabetic dogs, and showed a decline in blood sugar concentrations" (Williams and Pickup 2004, 10). We will discuss this in additional detail in the next section on the discovery of insulin. On the examination of this topic, we find that "the benefits of animal studies in diabetes research are illustrated most dramatically by the early studies of the dog over a century ago in which the induction of diabetes by pancreatectomy led to a realization of the role of the pancreas in insulin secretion. The successful extraction of insulin from the canine pancreas began the modern era in our understanding and treatment of diabetes" (Kahn and Weir 1994, 317). The affecting qualities of insulin in diabetes treatment have since been tested on mice and other animals to help doctors and scientists find the means to treat humans.

Despite its helpfulness, "the major limitation in the use of animal models is the lack of a perfect correlation between animal and human disease. No animal model has characteristics of diabetes identical to those in humans. Nevertheless, once a specific pathologic mechanism is fully understood in the diabetic animal, a similar defect may be found in diabetic humans, contributing to our knowledge of this disease in humans" (Kahn and Weir 1994, 318). Keeping this fact in mind is crucial to the development of diabetes treatment. In the next section, we will see the ways in which animal experimentation yielded one of the largest medical advancements of the twentieth century.

THE DISCOVERY OF INSULIN

The discovery of insulin was undoubtedly a major step forward in the field of diabetes research, but, like many roads, it was not a clear path of discovery. As is common in many fields of research, there are those who first discovered insulin and there are those who discovered insulin and were the first to be publicly recognized for their findings.

As early as 1909, insulin had been recognized as the previously unknown substance produced in the pancreas. A Belgian by the name of Jean de Meyer first proposed the name, which he derived from the Latin term for island, "insula." Through numerous tests and trials over the next decade, it became hard to "dispute the conclusion that the pancreas must have two functions. The digestive juices, poured into another organ, were the pancreas's *external* secretions. Its other function must be to produce some other substance, an *internal* secretion, which fed directly into the bloodstream and regulated carbohydrate metabolism" (Bliss 1982, 27). It was this internal secretion that drove many to test, in vain, their various theories to relate this pancreatic function to the cause of diabetes.

Twelve years later, "a Romanian biochemist, physiologist, and experienced researcher" named Nicolae Paulescu published an article describing his successful isolation of insulin, although he referred to it in his work as "pancreine" (Sanders 2001b, 42). In 1922, Paulescu obtained a patent for his discovery only to find that his work had been surpassed by others. In retrospect, it has been concluded that "pancreine probably contained insulin—so did the pancreatic extracts prepared by several earlier researchers, especially a German named Zuelzer—but it was the Canadians who made insulin suitable for the treatment of diabetes" (Bliss 1982, 16). Although the Canadians are most often accredited for the discovery of insulin, it is clear that their path was not an easy one. Like the others before them, the men involved faced a number of personal and professional hardships along the way.

A Canadian by the name of Frederick Banting was driven to find the purpose of the internal secretions of the pancreas, yet this was not his initial road to success (see Figure 1.4). After facing a good deal of hardship with a failing medical practice and a deteriorating personal life, these and other factors brought him to the University of Toronto, where he convinced a professor to allow him to test his hypotheses. The professor, J. J. R. Macleod, despite having numerous doubts in the wake of others' previous failures, granted Banting a place to do his research. Initially "Banting wanted to try to isolate the internal secretions 'to relieve glycosurea.' He seems to have been identifying diabetes with glycosurea in the traditional way, rather than referring to the newer notion of hyperglycemia as the important condition to be relieved" (Bliss 1982, 50). With this in mind, one can follow Banting on his road to discovery.

Now to understand Banting's processes, one must understand the nature of previous pancreatic research. Most of the research being done before this point was met with inconclusive results. Time after time, researchers tried to isolate the mysterious substance in the pancreas. It was understood that the islets of Langerhans, inside the pancreas, had some sort of relationship with this internal secretion. As discovered from animal research, the external secretions from

Figure 1.4. Frederick Banting was the first person to isolate insulin from the pancreas of a dog and also to use the extracted insulin to treat diabetes successfully. *Courtesy of The National Library of Medicine.*

the pancreatic ducts did not have a direct effect on the development of diabetes. Working off of this information, it became clear to researchers that "the health of the islets [of Langerhans] was the key variable in the genesis of diabetes" (Bliss 1982, 49). Blocking of the pancreatic ducts alone was not enough to induce diabetes in a living subject, and the discovery of a solid link between the islets and the development of diabetes allowed researchers to shift the focus of their work.

Even so, this shift led to numerous unsuitable conditions in the field of diabetes treatment. "High blood sugar, or hyperglycemia, had been recognized for many years as a *sine qua non* of the diabetic condition. Measurements of blood sugar had not usually been involved in diabetes therapy or research, however, because they were very difficult" (Bliss 1982, 40). Keeping this in mind, "the single most important development in diabetes research, next to Allen's diets, was the rapid improvement between about 1910 and 1920 in techniques for measuring blood sugar" (Bliss 1982, 40). In allowing the measurement of blood sugar to be tested for the development of diabetes research, scientists were able to test the effects of pancreatic excretions on blood sugar levels.

One such scientist, by the name of Israel Kleiner, was interested in this development of blood sugar research. His interest focused on "the speed with which injections of sugar normally disappeared from circulation (that is, were assimilated by the system)" (Bliss 1982, 40). Once one could determine the amount of time it took for blood sugar to disappear under normal circumstances, one could then begin to test that time against the addition of various pancreatic extracts. In 1919, Kleiner tested such extracts in depancreatized dogs. Using "solutions of ground fresh pancreas in slightly salted distilled water," Kleiner injected the dogs "with blood sugar readings taken before and after infusion and at later intervals," helping him to determine what role the pancreas played in the control of diabetes (Bliss 1982, 40, 41). All of his research showed a decline in blood sugar levels in the dogs. Furthermore, Kleiner took his research a step further to show that it was, in fact, the pancreatic solution that caused the decline by testing solutions based with other organs. He tested blood sugar levels as well as urine sugar levels to be absolutely sure that his findings were not the product of an unidentified factor.

Of these earlier tests, one problem remained on the road to discovering insulin. Many of the pancreatic extracts being tested, including the ones created by Kleiner and Paulescu, left the test subjects with undesirable side effects. Unfortunately, in the wake of World War I, many of these men were unable to finance studies large enough to reevaluate their findings and determine ways to reduce the toxic side effects of their extracts. This is where we return to Fredrick Banting.

In 1921, Banting paired up with Charles Best, a medical student and research assistant to Macleod. Together, the two men began numerous pancreatic tests on dogs to determine the role the internal secretions of the pancreas played in the control of diabetes development. The production of their extract involved putting sliced pieces of degenerated pancreas "into a chilled laboratory mortar containing ice-cold 'artificial blood' or Ringer's solution, a mixture of salts in water commonly used to preserve tissues. The mortar was put in a freezing brine solution until its contents partly froze. The half-frozen pancreas pieces were then macerated (ground up with sand and a pestle). The solution was filtered, apparently through cheesecloth and blotting paper, to eliminate the solid particles. The filtrate, a pinkish-coloured liquid extract of degenerated pancreas, was warmed to body temperature and was ready for injection" (Bliss 1982, 68). The men used degenerated pancreas because they believed that, by allowing the pancreas to deteriorate, it would damage the pancreatic ducts, thereby stopping the external secretions of the organ, allowing them to concentrate the internal secretions left in the pancreas. Even with this solid recipe for their extract, Banting and Best faced numerous setbacks in their research. Conducting tests on numerous dogs in their laboratory at the University of Toronto, many of the dogs died before the men could obtain any conclusive results they had hoped to yield from their work. After several failed attempts in research, their concoction, which they called "Isletin," successfully brought one of their test dogs out of a diabetic induced coma. Although the dog died soon after, their progress seemed to look a bit more promising. After that mild achievement, the men "made extracts from the liver and spleen of dogs, prepared them exactly the same way as the extracts of pancreas, and injected them into the collie [they'd been testing]. Neither caused any significant change in blood sugar. Injections of 'Isletin' later in the day gradually drove down the blood sugar," giving the men another small dose of success (Bliss 1982, 72). A year later, after endless experimentation, the concoction, newly named insulin, was presented at the Association of American Physicians. Welcomed with enthusiasm, insulin began its rounds as the first effective treatment of diabetes (see Figure 1.5).

Although early production of insulin proved a challenge, its triumphs far outweighed its drawbacks. Furthermore, in 1923, Banting and Macleod were awarded the Nobel Prize in Medicine or Physiology. Banting decided to share his portion of the prize with Best, and Macleod split his portion with James Collip, a biochemist he had hired to help with the isolation process. Rom this momentous achievement, medicine continued moving forward to the era of oral medication in diabetes treatment, which we will explore in the next section.

Figure 1.5. Insulin injections became a standard treatment for the management of diabetes. *Courtesy of The National Library of Medicine.*

THE DISCOVERY OF SULFONAMIDES

As you have seen with the discovery of insulin, the path to medical perfection is not an easy one to follow. The discovery of sulfonamides is not any clearer. Serious work on the development of the drugs began around the early part of the 1930s. It was not until almost a decade later that the drugs were discovered to be useful in the treatment of diabetes. It would be almost another decade more before they became readily available for public consumption.

Sulfonamides were originally developed by a German by the name of Gerhard Domagk in the 1930s. Domagk, "the director of research in experimental pathology and bacteriology at the German chemical firm I. G. Farben," conducted several experiments with the compound to test its ability to fight various strains of bacteria. There was a high rate of success in Domagk's experimentation, and the demand for the drugs skyrocketed through the following decade. In 1939, Domagk was presented with a Nobel Prize for his discovery, but he had to wait until the Nazis were removed from power before he was able to accept his award in 1947. Despite its popularity, "in the entire series of sulfonamides, so laboriously synthesized and tested, fewer than 20 clinically useful compounds were identified" (Magner 2005, 560). Furthermore, because sulfonamides were used often and in a careless manner, many of the bacteria they were supposed to combat developed strains resistant to the drugs.

One main feature of sulfonamides, which are made up of a sulfur compound, is that sulfonamides do not kill bacteria. Instead, the compound prevents the bacteria from reproducing, which, in turn, allows the body's immune system to rapidly target and destroy the infection. The usefulness of these drugs in the field of diabetes research began in the 1940s. In the early part of the decade, a professor of medicine at the University of Montpellier, Auguste Loubatières, made a critical discovery. While "studying the effects of long-acting insulin (IPZ) on depancreatized dogs, he observed prolonged low blood glucose levels (hypoglycemia), followed by convulsions, coma, and death" (Sanders 2001b, 51). At the same time, his colleague, Marcel Janbon, who "was studying how to use the bacteria-inhibiting sulfonamide drug 2254RP," provided Loubatières with interesting similarities in their work (Sanders 2001b, 51). In Janbon's studies, he found that three of the patients he treated had died from prolonged hypoglycemia. Over the next several years, Loubatières studied the effects sulfonamides had on the lowering of blood glucose levels. By 1946, Loubatières "concluded that sulfonamides exerted blood glucose-lowering effects by stimulating the pancreas to release insulin" (Sanders 2001b, 52). This major addition to the world of diabetes treatment was temporarily overshadowed in the wake of the war. Finally, in 1956, the first oral drug was released for the treatment of type 2 diabetes. The drug, called tolbutamide, was followed ten years later by "glibenclamide (glyburide), a more potent, prolonged-acting 'second generation' sulfonylurea" (Sanders 2001b, 52).

With this, we have established a solid basis for the history of diabetes research. From the earliest stages of chemistry in medical advancement to the monumental discoveries of the past century, it is without a doubt that diabetes research and treatment has come a long way.

2

Fundamental Principles

Mankind's struggle to understand the intricacies of diabetes was previously based on observation and speculation, without a firm understanding of its underlying causes. The Renaissance era led to remarkable cultural and scientific advancements, the results of which can still be seen to this day. Among these were milestones in basic sciences, such as anatomy and physiology. The many contributions over that past 3,500 years bring us to the modern definition of diabetes, which is based on the specific pathophysiology of the various subtypes of the disease.

Diabetes is a metabolic disorder, resulting in a disease process in which patients exhibit various symptoms as a result of hyperglycemia. In other words, the type of diabetes that someone has is associated with a specific physiological defect within the body that leads to high blood sugar (Powers 2004). Basic understanding of this concept is crucial to distinguishing between the different types of diabetes that exist and tailoring treatment in response to the different physiologic disturbances.

The number of people diagnosed with diabetes mellitus is on the rise, and the prevalence has increased from 8.9 to 12.3 percent in the past thirty years. Diabetes is a life-long disease that affects eighteen million Americans, with increasing numbers of people becoming susceptible because of lifestyle and poor eating habits (Pho 2005). However, it is not acceptable to categorize all diabetics as merely having "diabetes." Instead, a grouping system has been developed to distinguish between the different types of diabetes according to the specific physiologic disturbance that is leading to hyperglycemia. Many factors contribute to this metabolic dysfunction, including genetics, environment, and lifestyle. Although there are numerous types and subtypes of diabetes, we will focus on the three major types of diabetes: type 1, type 2, and gestational diabetes. By categorizing each class of diabetes, it becomes easier to study, diagnose, and treat accordingly.

The first grouping, type 1 diabetes, usually presents in childhood and is generally considered a disease of younger people. Although not as common as type 2 diabetes, type 1 comprises 10 percent of the diabetic population and is associated with more life-threatening conditions if not successfully maintained. Type 1 diabetics are distinguished from type 2 because they are insulin dependant, meaning that their bodies do not properly produce enough insulin to thrive. Until recently, these individuals have been burdened with daily insulin injections and constant monitoring of their food intake and exercise habits to remain symptom free. However, recent advancements such as the insulin pump are allowing type 1 diabetic patients to have a better quality of life. Type 1 diabetic patients are also at higher risk for medical emergencies than other diabetics because of their dependence on insulin and younger age of onset, hence the synonym, juvenile diabetes (Pho 2005).

Type 2 diabetes comprises 90 percent of the diabetic population and presents more commonly in adults than children. Unlike type 1 diabetes, which is defined by a lack of insulin, type 2 diabetes is associated with insulin resistance, meaning the body makes large amounts of insulin but the body does not recognize it. This leads to the hyperglycemia common to diabetics. A great emphasis on the etiology of type 2 diabetes is placed on sedentary lifestyle and poor eating habits, resulting in increased insulin produced to combat the high levels of glucose but with a lessened response. Initial treatment usually consists of lifestyle changes along with oral medications that can increase the body's sensitivity to insulin and help to control sugar levels within the bloodstream (Pho 2005).

The last major type of diabetes that we will discuss in this chapter is gestational diabetes. It is the least common of the three, effecting pregnant women. Women who develop gestational diabetes generally experience the first onset of hyperglycemia during the late stages of pregnancy, without any preexisting history of diabetes.

Distinguishing between the different types of diabetes is crucial to establishing a proper treatment regimen as well as focused research development.

Before we can discuss each of these types in more detail, we must first learn about how sugar is processed and used by the body and what can go wrong, leading to the different subtypes of diabetes. We will begin this chapter with the physiology and mechanisms of the human body and its relation to diabetes.

THE CELL: THE BASIC UNIT OF LIFE

Before we can discuss the pathophysiology of diabetes, we must first discuss the basic functions of various organ systems within the human body. Maintaining a proper energy balance within the human body is crucial for healthy existence. Whole food in its original form cannot be used by cellular

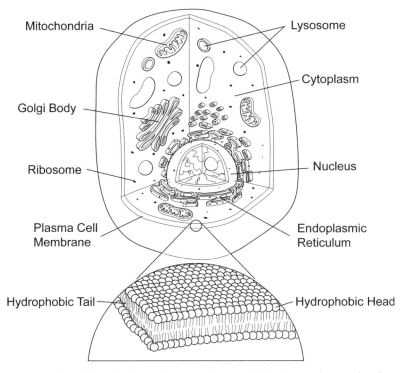

Figure 2.1. The cell is the basic functional unit of life that undergoes biochemical processes that require energy. Every cell contains various organelles that are required for the cell to function, including a centrally located nucleus that houses genetic material. It is encapsulated by a lipid bilayer that contains a hydrophobic (water-fearing) head and hydrophilic (water-loving) tail, which prevent molecules from entering and exiting. *Illustrator: Jeff Dixon.*

mechanisms and must be converted to other forms. The body breaks down ingested food into basic molecular structures that can be readily used by cells to create energy, allowing for life. These cellular processes take place in organs throughout the body, controlling how energy is expended and used (see Figure 2.1).

The human body is composed of trillions of cells. A cell is the smallest unit of living matter in which biochemical processes are performed. Considered to be the structural and functional units of all living organisms, cells come in many shapes and sizes according to the organ in which they are found and the function they perform. Because they are not visible to the human eye, scientists use microscopes as a tool to view and magnify the inner compartments of the cell. Light microscopes are used to view objects as small as 0.2 μm. An electron microscope can magnify to an even greater extent, making visible objects 0.002 μm in size. Cellular biology has expanded tremendously with the advent of these histological techniques.

There are three main classifications of cells, including prokaryotic, eukaryotic, and viruses. The tissues found within humans are composed of groups of eukaryotic cells. These cells are unique in that they contain a nuclear membrane and various membrane-bound organelles within the body of the cell. Bacterial cells, conversely, are grouped as prokaryotic and do not contain membranous structures. We will briefly discuss the function of eukaryotic cells and their role in diabetes.

One feature common to all cells in the human body is the cell membrane. The cell membrane forms the periphery of the cell, and it serves as a protective barrier to the inner organelles. The cell membrane is composed of a lipid bilayer that controls various substances from entering and exiting according to forces such as osmotic and electrochemical gradients. There are two layers to the cell membrane, an inner and an outer layer. The inner layer is composed of fatty acid chains, and the outer layer is composed of phospholipids. The resulting membrane is flexible, resilient, and can morph into various shapes without being damaged.

Proteins within the lipid bilayer form channels that carry molecules in and out of the cell. This allows the cell to control the internal milieu of the system, allowing only necessary molecules to enter. These channels allow substances to transverse the layers, similar to a tunnel that allows cars to pass across a body of water. Many of these channels are regulated by receptors that control the opening and closing of the passageway, much like a toll booth that ultimately controls what can or cannot enter. Receptors respond only to specific stimuli and are under tight control by substances known as ligands.

A ligand is a molecule or ion that binds to a protein receptor located on the cell membrane. There are many forces that determine whether a ligand will bind to a receptor, including ionic charges, van der Waals forces, and shape of the ligand and binding site. The shape of the ligand and binding site plays a very important role in chemical specificity. Complementary shapes will have a higher binding affinity, like a proper key for a lock. A ligand that activates one receptor will have no effect on another. With a specific system in place, the body is able to control various metabolic activities, such as glucose utilization, waste removal, and energy conservation.

There are two distinct compartments that can be found within the cell: the nucleus and the cytoplasm. The nucleus is found in the center of the cell and is surrounded by a nuclear envelope. The nucleus serves as a storage area for genetic information known as DNA, which performs functions such as protein synthesis and genetic expression of the cell. Genetic coding helps to differentiate and control cell function. Cells perform various tasks within the body with the guidance of genetics.

The cytoplasm surrounds the nucleus and contains organelles that are surrounded by a fluid known as cytosol. The various organelles within the cytoplasm perform specific tasks that allow the cell to thrive. The type of organelles found in the cell and the composition of the cytosol is determined by the genetic coding found in the DNA. The ratio of certain organelles within a cell allow for a specific function to be performed. The function of cells can be quite varied. For example, endocrine cells in the testes secrete testosterone, whereas nerve cells in the spinal cord release neurotransmitters.

Cells of similar function work together by linking to one another to form tissues. A tissue is a combination of similar cells that work together to perform a specific function. Muscle, for example, is a tissue that is composed of numerous cells that are involved in producing tension. There are four distinct classifications of specialized cell types, including epithelial, connective tissue, nerve, and muscle cells. Epithelial serves as a lining for organs, thereby separating the body into compartments. Connective tissue is responsible for providing proper support and structure. Ligaments and cartilage are examples of connective tissue and are strong and durable. Muscle tissue is specialized tissue with the main function of contraction. Contraction produces tension for moving limbs, controlling eye movement, and moving food through the digestive system. Nerve tissue is responsible for generating and conducting electrical signals from the brain and the spinal cord along nerves. Nerve tissue controls motor and sensory function. These various tissues provide a complex network of actions that result in a unified system.

Interestingly, two types of tissues can work together to form an organ. The heart, lung, liver, and pancreas are all examples of organs. An organ consists of distinct functional units that perform biological processes. For example, in the lung, the functional unit responsible for processing air is the alveoli. In the kidneys, the functional unit involved in filtering out toxic metabolites from the blood is the nephron.

An organ system is a combination of organs that perform a task. For example, the endocrine system is a combination of glands throughout the body that secrete hormones. There are ten organ systems within the human body that work in unison to perform functions that are essential for the survival of the organism. A series of chemical and electrical signals provide homeostasis and balance, otherwise known as "good health."

THE FATE OF FOOD

It is important to have a general understanding of the digestive system when discussing diabetes. Because cellular mechanisms involved in the body cannot utilize foodstuffs directly, a series of events must take place to process foods into smaller particles. The digestive system uses both mechanical and chemical means of breaking down ingested foodstuffs, with the end product being energy that drives processes of life. We will discuss this series of events by using the example of a piece of chocolate, following what happens within the human digestive system after it is eaten. We will focus on features that are important to our understanding of diabetes. We will use chocolate as an example mainly because of its high sugar content and will focus on the fate of this sugar.

A common chocolate bar consists of mainly sugar, cocoa, and milk. To be even more specific, we can think of chocolate as consisting of carbohydrates, proteins, and fats. Chocolate enters the oral cavity, or mouth, and is subjected to grinding by the teeth via the process of mastication, or chewing, which increases the surface area of the food. This increase in surface area allows for a greater amount of the food to be exposed to the action of the digestive enzymes of the stomach and the small intestines. In addition to the mechanical breakdown, the chocolate is subjected to salivary amylase, an enzyme that begins the chemical breakdown of carbohydrates. Eventually, the food is formed into a bolus that is swallowed with the aid of the tongue. The bolus travels down the esophagus and enters the stomach through peristaltic motion. This type of motion is caused by the action of skeletal and smooth muscles that contract in wavelike patterns to carry the food away from the mouth. Within the stomach, food is subjected to a very acidic environment and the enzyme pepsin. Protein degradation or breakdown begins when the food is exposed to these conditions. The bolus that entered the stomach exits the stomach mixed with acids and stomach secretions dubbed as chyme.

It is in the small intestine that most of the digestion and absorption of nutrients occurs. The chyme that enters the small intestine is subjected to many enzymes that are specific for the breakdown of carbohydrates, proteins, and fats. Many of these enzymes are secreted into the small intestine from other organs, including the liver and the pancreas. The liver is involved in secreting bile, which aids in fat absorption. The pancreas secretes many enzymes, but we shall focus mainly on the amylase. This amylase is similar to the one that was secreted in the oral cavity and is involved in the breakdown of carbohydrates into simple sugars known as monosaccharides. This degradation is necessary because the wall of the small intestine can only absorb monosaccharides; anything larger will not pass through. The polysaccharides are cleaved into smaller units by these amylases, taking the form of simple sugars. These sugars are able to enter the cells of the intestinal border and ultimately enter the nearby blood circulation.

As the sugar, or glucose, from the chocolate bar enters the bloodstream, signals are sent to the beta cells of the pancreas, stimulating the release of insulin into the bloodstream as well. The basic effect of insulin is to counteract the hyperglycemia by increasing glucose uptake into skeletal muscles or converting the glucose into a storage form known as glycogen.

The system is highly efficient in healthy individuals, and sugar levels are maintained within normal limits. However, a defect in any one of these mechanisms can lead to hyperglycemia. A decreased amount of insulin production by the pancreas will result in the sugar being "stuck" in the bloodstream until it is urinated out. In other forms of hyperglycemia, the response to insulin by muscle, fat, and liver cells can be decreased. This type of poor response is called insulin resistance or tolerance (Pho 2005).

THE DUALITY OF THE PANCREAS

The pancreas plays a part in both digestive and endocrine functions (see Figure 2.2). It is composed of two functionally distinct organs: the exocrine pancreas and the endocrine pancreas. The pancreas is located in the abdominal cavity behind the stomach. There are four sections of the pancreas distinguished by anatomic positioning to neighboring organs: the head, neck, body, and tail. The pancreatic duct is a tube that carries digestive enzymes into the small intestine. It receives its blood supply from nearby pancreaticoduodenal arteries and is innervated by a pancreatic plexus.

The exocrine pancreas secretes digestive enzymes directly into the intestines via the pancreatic duct, bypassing the systemic blood circulation (see Figure 2.3). Enzymes break down ingested food into smaller, absorbable

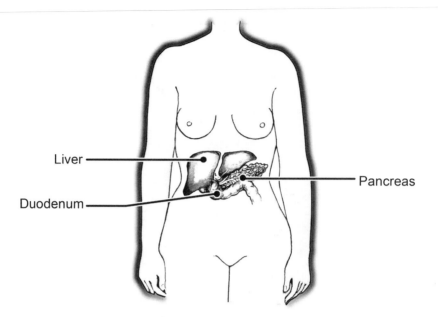

Figure 2.2. The pancreas is an organ located behind the stomach. The head of the pancreas is located within the curve of the duodenum. *Illustration courtesy of Michael Brookman.*

particles. Pancreatic amylase, lipase, trypsinogen, and chymotrypsinogen are enzymes that perform this function. As food is broken down, the small intestine absorbs nutrients into the portal circulation (Masharani, Karam, and German 2004).

The endocrine pancreas is unique in that its secretions enter the systemic circulation and effect tissues throughout the body. The hormones of the endocrine pancreas control cellular nutrition. Specifically, the endocrine pancreas alters the rate of absorption, cellular storage, and metabolism of sugars in the bloodstream. Any dysfunction related to these actions either from the pancreas or the target cells results in a metabolic disturbance known as diabetes (Masharani, Karam, and German 2004).

The endocrine pancreas is composed of approximately one million glands known as the islets of Langerhans. These islets can be found throughout the pancreas and contain four types of cells, including alpha, beta, delta, and pancreatic polypeptide cells. Most of the cells within the pancreas receive their blood supply from the celiac artery, whereas the posterior portion receive blood from the superior mesenteric artery (Masharani, Karam, and German 2004). The anterior, or front, portion of the pancreas contains predominantly

Common Bile Duct

Pancreatic Duct

Gallbladder

Pancreas

Duodenum

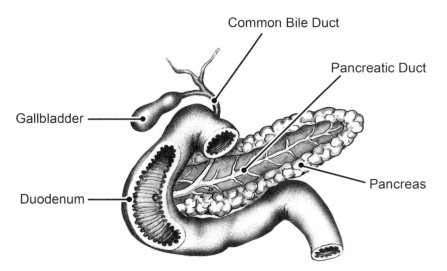

Figure 2.3. The exocrine pancreas secretes digestive enzymes into the pancreatic duct, which empties into the duodenum. The pancreatic duct joins the common bile duct before entering the duodenum. The endocrine pancreas secretes hormones directly into nearby blood vessels. *Illustration courtesy of Michael Brookman.*

beta cells. These cells comprise the majority of the islet cells, approximately 80 percent of the composition. Beta cells are involved in secreting a product known as insulin. The remaining 20 percent of the islet cells are formed by alpha cells, which produce glucagon. A very small percentage of cells known as delta cells are also found in the islets and secrete somatostatin (Masharani, Karam, and German 2004). The products of these cells will be discussed in detail later in this chapter.

On examination of the pancreas, it can be observed that the islets receive a large amount of blood supply compared with the exocrine glands that produce digestive enzymes. One islet cell receives enough blood flow to supply ten exocrine glands! The flow of blood from the islets is from a central to peripheral, or outer, direction. This flow mechanism allows for proper homeostasis and balance between insulin and glucagon secretion (Masharani, Karam, and German 2004).

INSULIN'S ROOTS AND ROUTES

The synthesis of insulin by the pancreatic beta cells begins with a precursor molecule known as pre-proinsulin. This molecule is used as a starting material by the cell. Enzymes found within the beta cells cleave, or breakdown, pre-proinsulin into the smaller molecule proinsulin. A small percentage of the breakdown product enters the bloodstream and is eventually filtered out by the kidneys. More importantly, the majority of the proinsulin is sent through several biochemical reactions within the Golgi apparatus in the cytoplasm of the cell. After cycling through these reactions, proinsulin is converted into C-peptide and insulin (Masharani, Karam, and German 2004).

C-peptide does not have any significant biological function in the control of glucose levels. However, it is known that C-peptide plays a minor role in preventing some long-term consequences of diabetes such as nerve and kidney damage. More importantly, it is beneficial in testing for diabetes. C-peptide levels are often measured by physicians to distinguish between type 1 and type 2 diabetics in patients with newly diagnosed diabetes. C-peptide is produced in a one to one ratio as insulin. However, when compared with insulin, C-peptide is removed from the body at a rate that is three times slower. This slower elimination rate serves to minimize the fluctuating effects of glucose, making it a good, stable test. For example, the amount of insulin that is found in the portal circulation at any time ranges from two to ten times the amount found in the systemic circulation attributable to metabolism by the liver. Conversely, C-peptide does not undergo this fluctuation and remains at a more constant level. Physicians are able to diagnose both type 1 and type 2 diabetes based on C-peptide levels rather than insulin levels. Type 1 diabetics have a C-peptide level that is decreased because the pancreas is unable to form insulin. In contrast, type 2 diabetics have C-peptide levels higher than normal as a result of high levels of insulin produced by the pancreas (Masharani, Karam, and German 2004).

Insulin is derived from the breakdown of proinsulin. Insulin is an endocrine substance used to control blood sugar levels throughout the day. It plays a major role in promoting a state of energy storage and conservation. Unlike C-peptide, insulin undergoes metabolism within the liver and removed at a faster rate from the body. After formation of insulin by the beta cells, insulin enters into the systemic circulation in specific concentrations determined by external variables such as food intake, glucose levels, and glucagon levels. The pancreas secretes an average of forty-five units of insulin per day. Levels of systemically secreted insulin begin to rise only eight minutes after ingestion of food because of increases in glucose and gastrointestinal secretions. Insulin levels reach their highest levels after approximately thirty minutes of ingesting a meal. During this peak of insulin, glucose exits the bloodstream and enters the cell, causing an overall decline in blood glucose. Proper function of this mechanism keeps blood glucose levels under 200 mg/dl after a meal. Declining glucose levels halt stimulation of the pancreatic beta cells, and insulin levels in

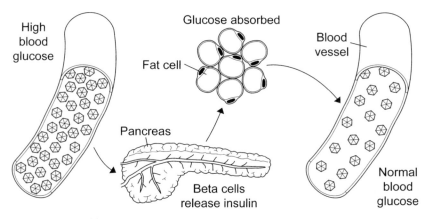

Figure 2.4. High blood glucose stimulates the beta cells of the pancreas to secrete insulin into the bloodstream. Insulin works on the liver to promote the conversion of free glucose to stored glycogen. A second effect of insulin is to drive glucose into the peripheral cells, further lowering the blood sugar level. *Illustrator: Jeff Dixon.*

the bloodstream return to a baseline, or normal, value. A baseline insulin level is achieved approximately one hour after cessation of stimulation. Baseline insulin value is defined as the amount of insulin found in circulation after fasting. For example, insulin levels are similar during a fasting period compared with ninety minutes after a meal (Masharani, Karam, and German 2004).

The major stimulant of insulin secretion is glucose (see Figure 2.4). After a meal, ingested foodstuff is broken down into smaller particles and utilized for energy by the body. Glucose is one of the end products of the actions of digestive system. It plays an intricate role in directly stimulating the pancreatic beta cells to secrete insulin. Categorized as a "direct" stimulant, glucose passes through the plasma membrane of the beta cell and initiates a series of biochemical reactions that result in the release of insulin (Masharani, Karam, and German 2004).

Besides glucose, other substances effect the secretion of insulin. Sulfonurea is another substance, like glucose, that also stimulates beta cells directly. Sulfonureas are used pharmacologically to increase insulin levels. They compensate for low levels of insulin in the diabetic condition. Indirect stimulants, conversely, amplify the direct actions of glucose on the beta cells. A simple experiment of comparison shows this relation. During normal ingestion of food, there is direct stimulation from glucose along with indirect stimulation by molecules produced by the metabolic processes of the digestive organs. Under these conditions, insulin levels rise a great deal because of synergism. Synergism occurs when two separate agents act together to create an effect greater than that produced separately by the individual agents. However, it is possible to minimize the actions of the indirect stimulants by avoiding their release. This can be achieved by bypassing the gastrointestinal system by injecting glucose directly into the bloodstream. Using this method, insulin levels rise at a slower rate and do not peak as high in a given time. There are many indirect stimulants that act via this mechanism, but discussing individual molecules is beyond the scope of this text. Along with the direct and indirect stimulators of insulin, there are also substances that inhibit pancreatic secretions. Precise control of insulin levels is attained through these mechanisms, allowing for the ultimate goal of storing glucose (Masharani, Karam, and German 2004).

Hormonal balance is maintained by feedback mechanisms. During episodes of increased glucose concentrations, beta cells release insulin and delta cells release somatostatin. Pancreatic alpha cells, however, are not affected directly by glucose levels. Rather, they are inhibited by the presence of insulin and glucagon. Alpha cells therefore are nonfunctioning during times of increased glucose. As levels of glucose decline, the reverse occurs and inhibition is released, much like releasing the brakes on a car. Without inhibition, alpha cells begin to secrete glucagon (see Figure 2.5). This networking of excitation and inhibition creates an environment that is ideal for good control of ingested glucose (Masharani, Karam, and German 2004).

Insulin exits the pancreas into the bloodstream, reaching various cells within the body. Along the way, insulin is exposed to receptors on fat, liver, and muscle cells. Insulin attaches to these receptors on cell membranes with

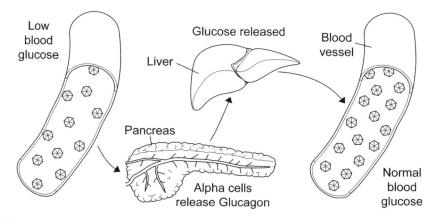

Figure 2.5. Low blood glucose triggers the alpha cells of the pancreas to release the hormone glucagon. Glucagon acts on the liver to stimulate the conversion of glycogen to glucose and releases it into the bloodstream. *Illustrator: Jeff Dixon.*

high affinity. The attachment occurs quickly with high specificity, meaning that only insulin can affect these receptors. Insulin is engulfed by the cell, or internalized, driving the cell into glycogen and fat synthesis. Once inside the cell, insulin initiates metabolic pathways that regulate the fate of sugar, specifically glycogen and lipid synthesis. Under these circumstances, the cell is directed toward a general state of energy conservation (Masharani, Karam, and German 2004).

The efficacy of insulin can be altered in many ways. The effects of insulin on the cell can be modified by two mechanisms: decreased numbers of receptors and decreased affinity of the receptors. Variables such as increased food intake and obesity can lead to chronically elevated levels on insulin, causing peripheral receptors to decrease in number. This process is called downregulation. Downregulation commonly occurs during states of chronically increased insulin levels attributable to external stimulation. Stimuli that lead to heightened levels include overeating and obesity, which is defined as increased body weight relative to height. A decreased number of insulin receptors in the periphery causes insulin to have less of an effect in controlling glucose levels. This leads to a faulty glucose control mechanism, leading to hyperglycemia (Masharani, Karam, and German 2004).

The effects of insulin on blood glucose can also be altered by decreasing the actual amount of insulin produced by the body. Inhibitor molecules such as somatostatin, or even episodes of heavy exercise and decreased food intake cause a decline in insulin levels. Hormonal stimulation by the adrenal cortex can also alter the binding affinity of insulin to peripheral cells. A reduction in the amount of insulin found within the circulation allows for energy to be utilized rather than stored (Masharani, Karam, and German 2004).

The mechanism that is most susceptible to creating insulin resistance can be found within the cell. After insulin passes through the cell membrane, a series of biochemical pathways are activated (see Figure 2.6). These pathways change the structure of the cell membrane and allow glucose to enter. Examples of internalized processes include insulin activity and glucose receptor movement toward the cellular membrane. Abnormal reaction function within the cytoplasm can build resistance, leading to a decreased efficacy of peripherally found insulin (Masharani,, Karam, and German 2004).

Successful binding and intracellular modification of insulin leads to biological effects, resulting in the uptake of glucose. Glucose receptors, or channels, form in the cellular membrane to allow for the passage of glucose into the cytoplasm of the cell. Once within the cell, glucose undergoes a series of changes and is converted to a storage form known as glycogen (Masharani, Karam, and German 2004).

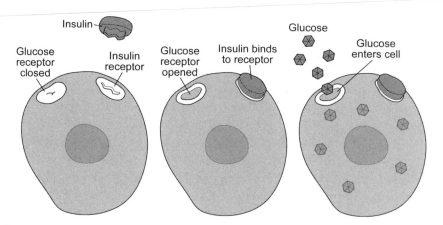

Figure 2.6. Left, the lipid bilayer contains the glucose channel and the insulin receptor. The glucose channel is closed in its resting state. Center, when insulin is released from the pancreas, it binds to the insulin receptor, causing the glucose channel to open. Right, with the glucose channel open, glucose is able to enter the cell, thereby lowering the blood glucose level. *Illustrator: Jeff Dixon.*

Insulin induces changes in the function of the liver. The liver is found in the upper right quadrant of the abdomen and is involved in storing energy and detoxification. One of the main functions of the liver is converting glucose to glycogen. Think of the liver as a factory that processes, packages, and stores glucose in a more compact form called glycogen. Nutrient-rich blood from the intestine is sent to the liver via portal circulation. Depending on the status of the body (fed or fasting), the liver processes glucose accordingly. The liver can also reverse the process and convert the glycogen into glucose to be used as a source of energy. The liver stores approximately half a day's worth of glycogen to meet the demands of the fasting body (Masharani, Karam, and German 2004).

Under the effects of insulin, the liver drives the reaction to convert glucose to glycogen. The conversion of glucose to glycogen is a form of anabolism. The process of anabolism is defined as a chemical reaction that causes various smaller molecules to combine and form larger more complex forms (Paustian 2000). The liver acts as a sponge to take up a large percentage of glucose under the influence of insulin. Once within the liver cell, or hepatocyte, glucose undergoes several biochemical reactions, activating several of the enzymes that are directly involved in glycogen synthesis, including phosphofructokinase and glycogen synthase (Masharani, Karam, and German 2004).

In addition to glycogen synthesis, insulin also stimulates the formation of proteins, lipids, and triglycerides within the liver. Products of these reactions provide an alternate source of energy storage that can be measured in calories. The measurement of energy within the body is referred to as calories. One calorie is chemically defined as the amount of energy it takes to raise the temperature of one cubic centimeter of water by one degree Centigrade. Scientists measure energy in the form of kilocalories (kcal), which is equivalent to one thousand calories. Running one mile will utilize approximately 100 kcal. One gram of protein can store 4 kcal of energy. Proteins are also essential for the well being of an individual and drive many biological processes. Lipids can store greater than two times the energy as proteins. Lipids are considered to be fat soluble, meaning that they cannot be dissolved in a water solution. They are derived from fatty acids, which can join together to form various substances such as cholesterol, fat, and even parts of the cellular membrane (Masharani, Karam, and German 2004). One gram of fat is capable of storing 9 kcal of energy. This form of storage allows energy to be stored in a more compact and efficient manner.

Besides stimulating reactions that increase glycogen, protein, and lipid levels, insulin is also involved in inhibiting those processes that break them down. The chemical reaction that is responsible for converting glycogen into glucose is halted under the influence of insulin. These effects inhibit catabolism. A catabolic process can be defined as a series of biochemical reactions that are involved in taking a large molecule and converting it into smaller molecules, with the end result being the release of energy. Insulin inhibits the conversion of fatty acids into keto acids and also inhibits the conversion of amino acids into glucose (Masharani, Karam, and German 2004).

Within muscle, insulin has anabolic effects on the tissues. The first effect of insulin is that it enters muscle cells and undergoes a series of reactions that form glucose channels on the cellular membrane. Glucose that is in the circulation can now enter the cell. Once inside, glucose is converted to glycogen under the continued stimulation of insulin. This conversion allows muscle tissues to replenish and restore their reserves of glycogen to be utilized for energy expenditure later. Muscle is considered to be one of the largest reserves of glycogen within the body because of the large percentage of body weight that muscle makes up. The liver, however, stores more glycogen per gram of tissue when compared with muscle tissue. Contraction of skeletal muscle reverses this reaction, thereby stimulating glycogenolysis. Glycogenolysis provides additional energy to the muscle tissue. Unlike the liver, however, muscle tissue cannot perform the reverse chemical reaction, making it impossible for muscles to directly replenish blood levels of glucose. This is attributable to a lack of certain enzymes necessary that are found mainly in the liver and not in muscle. Despite this fact, the end process of energy utilization by the muscle tissue produces byproducts that enter the circulation to be processed by the liver (Masharani, Karam, and German 2004).

Fat is considered the ultimate form of energy storage. Under the influence of insulin, lipogenesis takes place within adipose tissue. Lipogenesis promotes storage of fatty acids and simultaneously inhibits the release of fatty acids from the cell. Insulin binds to the fat cell and changes the configuration of the cellular membrane, allowing for glucose to enter. In addition to glucose uptake, the cells also produce an enzyme called lipoprotein lipase that is involved in triglyceride uptake from the circulation. The overall effect is an increased amount of energy stores within the cell and decreased levels within the bloodstream (Masharani, Karam, and German 2004).

Glucose enters different types of cells by mechanisms unique to each. As we discussed earlier, the cell membrane is composed of a lipid bilayer that prevents the passage of water-soluble molecules. Glucose is categorized as hydrophilic, or water loving. This means that glucose can form bonds with water along with other polar or charged liquids. An example of this hydrogen binding property is seen when sugar is mixed with water and fully dissolves. One cup of water combined with a cup of table sugar will form one cup of solution (not two) because of solubility factors. Because the lipid bilayer has nonpolar portions, glucose needs to be carried or escorted into the cell via transport mechanisms. These transport mechanisms bypass the block created by the cell membrane (Masharani, Karam, and German 2004).

One example of a glucose transporter is GLUT 1. GLUT 1 receptors are found throughout the body in every tissue and allow for the passage of glucose through the cell membrane. The major defining characteristic of GLUT 1 receptors is that they have a very high affinity for glucose. Under these conditions, glucose enters the cell even at very low systemic concentrations. A high affinity for glucose is especially important in structures such as the blood brain barrier, because glucose is the brain's main source of energy. Even at basal or baseline levels, glucose enters and adequately supplies the cells of the central nervous system. Along with GLUT 1, GLUT 3 is found predominately in the nervous system and allows for glucose transport into neuronal cells (Masharani, Karam, and German 2004).

Cells of the liver, intestines, and kidneys predominately contain GLUT 2 receptors. These receptors are most active after a nutrient-rich meal during high concentrations of glucose within the bloodstream. GLUT 2 receptors have a very low affinity to glucose when compared with GLUT 1. It has been shown that, as the levels of glucose increase, the amount entering through the GLUT 2 receptors increases as well. This is a mechanism well suited for rapid glucose storage by the liver, which is inhibited when there are low levels of glucose (Masharani, Karam, and German 2004).

Skeletal muscle and adipose cells (fat cells) contain high concentrations of GLUT 4 receptors. GLUT 4 receptors are not found on the surface of the cell membranes of the cell; rather, they are found internally in the cytoplasm. Insulin chemically stimulates GLUT 4 receptors to migrate to the periphery of the cell and penetrate the cell membrane, thereby accommodating the passage of glucose. These receptors play an important role in internalizing glucose for eventual storage and conversion to glycogen (Masharani, Karam, and German 2004).

GLUCAGON

Glucagon is a molecule that has an important role in controlling blood glucose levels. When compared with insulin, glucagon has a physiological function that counteracts and opposes energy conservation. Insulin can be thought of as molecule that controls and reduces blood glucose levels by making it available to cells and stimulating storage. Glucagon, conversely, performs the opposite task and is used by the body when there is decreased amounts of glucose in the bloodstream and when there are increased energy needs (Masharani, Karam, and German 2004).

The alpha cells of the islets of Langerhans form glucagon. Glucagon is derived from a precursor molecule that is much larger known as proglucagon. Along with glucagon, glucagon-like peptide 1 (GLP-1) and GLP-2 are also released but have no effect on insulin secretion. After a twelve hour fast, glucagon levels within the bloodstream rise dramatically, and levels actually double by the third day of fasting. Although still under debate, the mechanism of release of glucagon during a fast can be attributable to two mechanisms or a combination of the two. Alpha cells are inhibited by the presence of large amounts of glucose. During times of fasting, glucose levels within the circulation plummet and inhibition of the alpha cells is removed, thereby releasing glucagon. Alpha cells are also inhibited directly by insulin and indirectly by glucose. Insulin levels rise during periods of increased glucose, thereby inhibiting glucagon secretion. As glucose levels drop, insulin levels drop and the alpha cells secrete glucagon (Masharani, Karam, and German 2004).

Glucagon performs the major task of making energy available for cellular processes necessary to sustain life. The liver is the main organ that is affected by the secretions of the alpha cells. Hepatocytes break down glycogen that was previously formed and storage reserves are depleted. Glucagon stimulates cells to drive reactions that increase levels of glucose in the body. Gluconeogenesis, or formation of new glucose, is an outcome of glucagon exposure to the cell. In this biochemical reaction, amino acids are converted into the more readily used form of energy. Along with stimulating glucose formation, glucagon also simultaneously inhibits processes that form triglycerides (Masharani, Karam, and German 2004).

The mechanisms that occur within the pancreas are normal biological processes that function normally to produce a balanced form of energy control. The physiology discussed above relates to principles of chemical signaling and feedback mechanisms that depend on the presence or absence of certain molecules within the system. Exocrine functions of the islet cells of the pancreas can be manipulated through stimulation by glucose, direct and indirect control mechanisms. Insulin drives the body to store energy in the form of glycogen, whereas glucagon opposes these actions and makes energy available via breakdown of larger molecules. Alteration in any of these mechanisms leads to poor control of blood glucose and causes secondary problems that can be associated with these defects. Pathology, or presence of disease, occurs when any of these functions are ineffective at performing proper physiological demands of the body. We will continue our discussion with the basic workings of the digestive system, pathology of diabetes, and specific mechanisms that cause disease (Masharani, Karam, and German 2004).

HOW SWEET IT IS: HYPERGLYCEMIA

A faulty insulin mechanism, either through production or utilization, leads to many short-term and long-term problems that are commonly experienced in diabetes. Some short-term complications include symptoms that were properly described thousands of years ago, including increased urination, increased thirst, and fatigue. Increased urination is caused by the abundance of glucose within the bloodstream that "overflows" into the urine. Excess glucose in the urine is cleared by the action of the kidneys. Excessive amounts of water is lost with this clearing as a function of the kidneys. Because of continuous fluid loss through the urinary system, thirst and compensatory drinking are experienced. Lethargy and fatigue are also commonplace. This is a result of the inability of sugars to effectively pass from the bloodstream into the cells that need it. The cells experience significantly low levels of glucose and are unable to generate the energy needed to thrive. In effect, the human body as a whole is affected with the outcome of glucose starvation despite the abundance found in the bloodstream (Pho 2005).

Hyperglycemia, or high blood glucose, is common to all diabetics and is the end result of dysfunctional processes of insulin secretion, glucose usage, and glucose production. The differences in etiology determine the type of diabetes that one can have, and it is of utmost importance that the distinction is made between the various causes of this infliction. Type 1 diabetes is characterized by a lack of insulin attributable to deficiency or defect. Most people with type 1 diabetes are under the age of thirty and are dependant on insulin therapy. Type 2 diabetes comprise a much larger percentage of diagnosed individuals and have varying degrees of pathologies of insulin and glucose management. Most patients with type 2 are over the age of forty and have underlying obesity (Pho 2005).

If diabetes goes untreated for an extended period of time, long-term complications can take their toll on the body. Neurological and vascular problems are the most common and are caused by prolonged hyperglycemia. Commonly involved areas include the eyes, kidneys, nerves, heart, gums, and feet. It is important to note that these complications are very serious and can occur inconspicuously without awareness of the problems. It is possible to reduce the risk and even prevent the occurrences of these problems with proper management of diabetes (Pho 2005).

Knowing the pathway that sugars take within the body will make it much easier to make a transition into learning about the different types of diabetes and their complications. We will continue with the next chapter by discussing type 1, type 2, and gestational diabetes in regards to compromised areas within the body along with risk factors and management.

3

Dissecting Diabetes: A Closer Look

TYPE 1 DIABETES

Type 1 diabetes comprises 10 percent of the diabetic population and is commonly diagnosed in children that have a genetic predisposition to developing this autoimmunity. Although the disease can also occur in adulthood, a greater percentage of children, nearly 1 of 500 children, are diagnosed with type 1 diabetes. Type 1 diabetes was previously referred to descriptively as juvenile diabetes or insulin-dependant diabetes. These names are now outdated because they are merely generalizations and do not describe the nature of the pathology. Therefore, a more accurate definition of type 1 diabetes describes the destruction of beta cells within the pancreas. Destruction of these cells can be attributable to a mounted autoimmune response or idiopathic reasons. Combinations of environmental and genetic factors determine an individual's susceptibility for developing type 1 diabetes. It is not uncommon for beta cell destruction to begin months to years before the development of diabetic signs and symptoms. The complete destruction of beta cells in the pancreas makes these patients dependant on scheduled insulin injections to control their hyperglycemia and to prevent complications (Kahn 2007).

An autoimmune disease process occurs when the body fails to recognize its own cells as self, resulting in a defensive attack against its own cells. The body uses its own immune system to wrongfully attack native cells until they are completely destroyed. It is now known that autoimmune responses are linked to genetic factors, affecting numerous genes within the genetic composition of the individual. However, even genetically susceptible individuals can never show signs of autoimmunity because of other factors such as environment and lifestyle. This being said, we can take for example monozygotic twins that are genetically identical and find that only 30 percent of these twins show signs of type 1 diabetes (Kahn 2007).

Type 1 diabetes is caused by the autoimmune process described above, affecting specific cells of the pancreas. The body flags the beta cells of the pancreas as foreign and mounts an immunologic attack against its own cells, leading to a dramatic decline in insulin production. The destroyed beta cells are unable to produce insulin, putting the body at a handicap against controlling fluctuations in glucose after meals. Insulin is a pertinent part of the mechanism of displacing sugar from the blood into peripheral cells. Furthermore, because insulin is not secreted into the bloodstream after ingesting a meal, the sugars in the bloodstream cannot be utilized by cells throughout the body. The end result is a hyperglycemic state, or diabetes (Kahn 2007).

Type 1 diabetes can be divided into two subtypes known as type 1A and type 1B diabetes mellitus. The prevalence of type 1A diabetes is greater than that of type 1B. Type 1A diabetes is caused by an autoimmune response that ultimately destroys pancreatic beta cells in the body. Type 1A diabetes is caused by numerous contributory factors such as genetics, environment, and immune response. The autoimmune response that is involved triggers an attack against the pancreas, leading to a steady decline in beta cell mass. The onset of type 1A is gradual, leading to beta cell death that occurs over months to years. Gradual decline in cell numbers allow for the disease process to go unnoticed by the individual until a threshold is reached. Glucose levels remain normal during this period of cell destruction because of the body's ability to compensate for the pathology. Symptoms do not become apparent until almost 80 percent of the beta cells are destroyed. With less than 20 percent of the normal cell remaining, a pathologic threshold is reached, and the body is unable to effectively manage blood glucose levels. The lack of these beta cells decreases the body's insulin production rate, causing a deficiency. As the disease progresses further, even more pancreatic beta cells are eliminated and a dependency for insulin develops (Powers 2004).

Type 1B diabetes mellitus is described as an insulin-dependant state without signs of an autoimmune process. Individuals with this subtype would test negative for antibodies that were positive for type 1A (islet cell antibodies, anti-glutamic acid decarboxylase [GAD], anti-insulin). These results lead us to term this disease process as idiopathic, or as having an unidentified cause. The majority of individuals that develop type 1B diabetes are from African, Hispanic, and Asian origin, composing a small percentage of type 1 diabetics. Despite the difference in causes, both type 1A and type 1B diabetics are considered to be insulin dependant and experience similar signs of hyperglycemia and dangerous episodes of ketoacidosis (Powers 2004).

Latent autoimmune diabetes of adulthood (LADA) is another subtype of type 1 diabetes that affects individuals over the age of thirty. These patients are sometimes mistakenly diagnosed with type 2 diabetes because of their late age of onset. However, laboratory tests for autoantibodies that suggest an autoimmune process establish a diagnosis of type 1 LADA. A second indication for the diagnosis of LADA is the lack of peripheral insulin resistance that is common to type 2 diabetes. These signs are important when establishing a treatment regimen, because management differs substantially. The onset of LADA is gradual, eventually leading to the total destruction of the pancreatic beta cells as in type 1A and 1B diabetes. The end result is a dangerous hyperglycemic state that must be prevented through medicinal intervention (Powers 2004).

The destructive autoimmune forces on the pancreas cause a decline in the number of properly functioning pancreatic beta cells (see Figure 3.1). When considering the pathophysiology of type 1 diabetes, it is important to recall

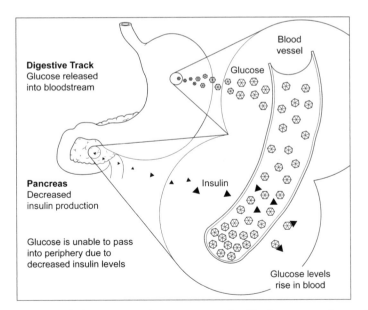

Figure 3.1. Type 1 diabetes. Hyperglycemia is a result of little or no insulin production by the pancreas. *Illustrator: Jeff Dixon.*

the mechanism of action of insulin. As we discussed previously, insulin is responsible for an anabolic process that allows cells to convert glucose and other molecules into larger forms for storage of energy.

A lack of insulin causes metabolic processes in the cells to favor energy expenditure, causing what we call an catabolic state. Glucose entering the systemic circulation is unable to produce a stimulatory response, and insulin is not secreted because of the decrease in beta cell numbers. Liver, muscle, and fat cells are all affected by this condition, and energy storage processes are reversed. Formation of glycogen is inhibited, and processes of catabolism are stimulated. Without insulin, GLUT 4 receptors cannot migrate to the lipid bilayer, making it impossible for glucose to enter the cell. The remaining glucose backs up and builds up in the bloodstream. With levels increasing constantly from the digestive process, a condition of hyperglycemia prevails (Masharani, Karam, and German 2004).

When considering feedback mechanisms, it is important to remember the relationship between insulin concentrations and glucagon secretion. Insulin is a potent inhibitor of the pancreatic alpha cells, which are responsible for the secretion of glucagon. Decreased levels of insulin in a type 1 diabetic remove inhibition from the alpha cells and cause them to secrete glucagon. The cells of the liver, muscles, and fat all respond to low insulin and high glucagon levels in certain ways. First, there is an increased delivery of glucose, amino acids, and fatty acids into the bloodstream. This is counterproductive because of the already high levels of blood glucose and contributes to the already present hyperglycemia. Second, large fat molecules are broken down into molecules known as ketones, which can accumulate to dangerous levels within the bloodstream (Masharani, Karam, and German 2004).

HYPERGLYCEMIA

The increased levels of glucose and fatty acids in the circulation cause certain functional changes that are characteristic to type 1 diabetes. Osmosis is a process that is affected by hyperglycemia. Osmosis is the process in which substances pass through a membrane that separates two solutions that have varied concentrations. We can visualize osmosis at work if we take two containers and separate them with a semi-permeable membrane. Container A contains pure water, and container B contains water and sugar. Over time, water passes through the membrane and flows from container A to container B. These similar events occur within the body as a result of hyperglycemia, particularly within the kidneys (see Figure 3.2).

The kidneys are responsible for controlling proper water balance and filtration of the circulating blood. A kidney can be found on either side of the

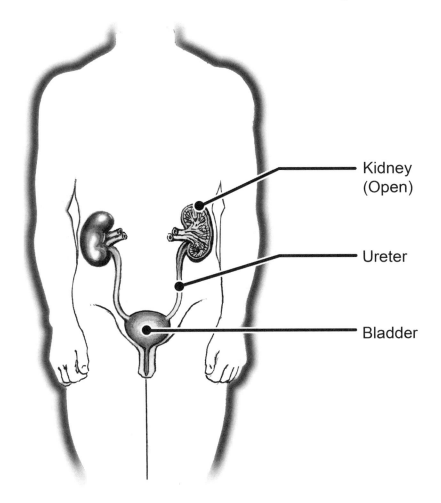

Kidney
(Open)

Ureter

Bladder

Figure 3.2. The kidneys are located in the retroperitoneal cavity. The kidneys form urine that travels down the ureter to collect in the bladder. *Illustration courtesy of Michael Brookman.*

posterior portion of the body just below the ribcage and are approximately the size of your fist. The kidneys play an integral role in processing and clearing waste products from the bloodstream. Approximately 200 quarts of blood are filtered by the kidneys per day, of which only two quarts are removed in the form of urine. Filtered urine flows from the kidneys into the bladder via the ureters. It is in the bladder that the urine gets stored until actual urination occurs. Proper removal of harmful materials is achieved by passage of blood through a filtration system within the renal tubules and furthermore through a series of tubules that are permeable to certain molecules (Dionne 2002).

The functional or most basic unit of the kidney is the nephron. Each nephron contains anatomic machinery that acts as an efficient filtration unit composed of a blood vessel and a renal tubule. Through a series of biochemical reactions based on concentration gradients and permeability gradients, the nephrons "strain" out harmful or unnecessary molecules from those that the body can still utilize (National Kidney and Urologic Diseases Information Clearinghouse 2005).

The kidneys are so efficient at their task that a human can live a healthy life with only 50 percent of their kidney function intact. This is why people are able to donate their kidneys for transplants. However, if the kidney function begins to drop significantly, toxins and other harmful materials can build up in the system instead of being filtered and eliminated. Patients with decreased kidney function will require dialysis treatment or even a kidney transplant (National Kidney and Urologic Diseases Information Clearinghouse 2005).

Hyperglycemia can cause an osmotic diuresis in a diabetic patient. Increased glucose levels in the bloodstream for prolonged periods of time have an effect on the osmolar gradient in the kidney (Masharani, Karam, and German 2004). As we have seen from the example of the two containers, water flows from an area of low concentration to an area of high concentration. In the nephron, more water is eliminated to compensate for the increased glucose concentration. This results in an increased production of urine and an increased frequency of urination.

With the loss of such massive amounts of water, the body tries to compensate by signaling thirst mechanisms. A classic complaint of diabetics is that they frequently urinate and are constantly thirsty. Children with type 1 diabetes are often diagnosed with the disease because of ongoing nighttime urination (Feld 2006).

In addition to the increased urination and thirst, diabetics also complain of blurred vision and difficulty seeing clearly. The eye has two compartments that are divided into the anterior, or front, and posterior, or back. The anterior compartment contains a fluid called the aqueous humour, and the posterior eye contains the vitreous humour. A high level of glucose in the circulation creates a hyperosmolar state within the eyes that affects both the retina and the lens, which are involved in focusing and receiving light (Masharani, Karam, and German 2004).

Weight loss is commonly found in type 1 diabetics because of decreased glucose utilization and increased diuretic effect of hyperglycemia. Diabetics lose much of their weight through the increased urine production of the kidneys. A state of chronic dehydration persists, and water weight cannot be maintained without proper medications. In addition to water loss, type 1 diabetics cannot process and metabolize sugars properly because they do not produce enough insulin. Cells are deprived of sugar and must seek alternative forms of creating energy. The body breaks down its own muscle and fat cells to compensate for the lack of sugar-processing capability. As muscle cells are used for their protein reserves, body mass gradually declines and weight loss occurs (Masharani, Karam, and German 2004).

The nervous system is also affected by hyperglycemia, and diabetic patients usually present with complaints of a sensation of numbness and tingling in their extremities, usually in their hands and feet. Neurons are the basic functional unit of the nervous system and contain a cellular membrane. High levels of glucose produce a form of reversible neurotoxicity attributable to the osmotic forces at work. On normalization of glycemic levels, however, symptoms of numbness usually subside (Briscoe and Davis 2006).

Type 1 diabetics are prone to displaying signs of ketoacidosis if their condition is not properly controlled. Many diabetics that are unaware of their condition are at risk for developing ketoacidosis. Diabetic ketoacidosis occurs then levels of insulin drop to a very low level, and the compensating breakdown of amino acids produces ketone bodies in high amounts. Increased levels of ketones are toxic to the body, and vomiting occurs along with altered mental status such as a stupor or even coma. It is common to smell acetone on the breath of a patient with ketoacidosis (Masharani, Karam, and German 2004).

TYPE 1 DIABETES: RISK FACTORS

Despite the numerous advances in understanding the mechanisms of insulin production and diabetic states, the causes of diabetes are still not completely understood. Type 1 diabetes is thought to occur because of genetic factors inherited by the offspring of the parent generation. Studies show that there is a significant correlation between an individual having a family history of diabetes and developing type 1 diabetes. There is a 6 percent increase in risk if a parent or sibling has type 1 diabetes. Likewise, this risk increases substantially if both groups show diabetic signs. Risk can also be accounted for by analyzing the effects of ethnicity on developing type 1 diabetes. In the United States, for example, Caucasians were found to have the highest correlation with type 1 diabetes. Taking a world survey, it can be seen that individuals from Finland and Sardinia have the highest rate of incidence. In contrast, Asians and Pacific Islanders were found to be the least effected groups. Correlations such as these can be used to estimate an individual's susceptibility for acquiring diabetes. These clues can allow physicians to determine those patients that are most at risk and begin monitoring pancreatic function and blood sugar before potential onset of type 1 diabetes (Kahn 2007).

The risk of developing type 1 diabetes also increases when another autoimmune disease state affects the body. For example, thyroid disease and celiac disease are two autoimmune diseases that have been linked with an increased susceptibility to type 1 diabetes. Celiac disease is an autoimmune process that damages the lining of the small intestine when exposed to certain proteins found in wheat products, specifically gluten. A study that was conducted in Sweden found that children diagnosed with celiac disease were three times more likely to develop type 1 diabetes when compared with the rest of the population. Supportive evidence for this correlation was also found in a Danish study that examined children with type 1 diabetes who were later diagnosed with celiac disease. It was determined that the previously undiagnosed celiac disease was asymptomatic before the onset of diabetes (Kahn 2007).

Thyroid disease is another factor that is closely associated with type 1 diabetes. Thyroid disease is an endocrine disorder that alters the body's rate of metabolism. Increase thyroid function is referred to as hyperthyroidism, whereas deceased function is termed hypothyroidism, with metabolism increasing and decreasing, respectfully. Because individuals with one autoimmune disease are susceptible to acquiring another, we can find a great correlation between type 1 diabetes and thyroid disease. One-third of type 1 diabetics have thyroid disease, which can have significant effects on blood glucose. Presence of thyroid disease can give clues to physicians to identify patients at high risk for developing type 1 diabetes (Kahn 2007).

Besides genetics and underlying autoimmune disease, type 1 diabetes can also be provoked by external environmental factors such as viruses or chemicals. This explains why many people who have a high genetic susceptibility to acquiring diabetes never experience any diabetic symptoms. Researchers are now trying to find specific environmental factors that can trigger the onset of diabetes, looking specifically at toxins, infectious agents, and diet types. Dr. William Hagopian, the leader of a study being conducted by the National Institute of Digestive and Diabetes and Kidney Diseases (NIDDK), is studying the experiences of diabetic patients over a span of twenty years in hopes to better understand these external triggers. Previous studies connected exposure to diary products and virus during the first several months of life to type 1 diabetes. Latent diabetes can be provoked by viruses that attack on the immune system, including Coxsackie B, enterovirus, adenovirus, rubella, cytomegalovirus, and Epstein Barr virus. In 2005, an experiment was conducted on mice to see the effects of virus-induced diabetes. Two groups of mice were infected with an encephalomyocarditis virus. One group was given immunosuppressive therapy, whereas the other group was exposed to only the virus. It was found that the mice exposed only to the virus had higher mean glucose levels. The mice that were given an immunosuppressant did not experience any changes in blood glucose. This study shows that an external trigger, here a virus, mounts an immunological response that triggers the onset of hyperglycemic states. Exposure to mothers breast milk for at least three months decreases the risk of developing diabetes. Another correlation linked exposure of cow milk during the first year of life to type 1 diabetes (Kahn 2007).

The goal of these research efforts is to isolate environmental triggers in hopes to take a preventative role against type 1 diabetes. Certain triggers such as wheat products and cows milk should be avoided during the first years of life. In addition to modifying diet by avoiding certain ingestible triggers, researchers are hoping to prevent the effects of viruses as well. Dr. Hagopian suggests the use of vaccinations against common viruses as a preventative measure against a future onset of diabetes. The steps that researchers are now taking in finding the cause of diabetes are the first of many that will lead to new developments in prevention and treatment in the future (Kahn 2007).

Although type 1 diabetes comprises only a small percentage of the diabetic population, there is an abundant amount of resources available to help manage and control this disease process. The quality of life of a type 1 diabetic has drastically improved because of advances in early diagnosis, accessible blood glucose monitoring, and insulin therapy. The future of medicine will open new doors in prevention and treatment of this autoimmune disease, which will be discussed in later chapters.

TYPE 2 DIABETES

Type 2 diabetes is the more prevalent type of diabetes, comprising about 90 percent of individuals diagnosed with diabetes. Type 2 diabetes was previously known as adult-onset diabetes and non-insulin-dependent diabetes, but these terms are now outdated. Individuals that are diagnosed with type 2 diabetes are commonly found to be over the age of forty with underlying obesity. Many of these diabetics are characterized as having a sedentary lifestyle and poor diet. Although the majority of type 2 diabetics are over the age of forty, younger individuals are at risk because of an increased frequency of obesity and sedentary lifestyle. The involvement of younger age groups makes the term adult-onset diabetes obsolete (Kahn 2007).

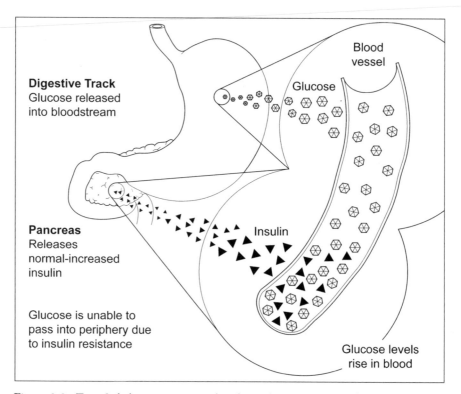

Blood vessel

Digestive Track
Glucose released
into bloodstream

Glucose

Pancreas
Releases
normal-increased
insulin

Insulin

Glucose is unable to
pass into periphery due
to insulin resistance

Glucose levels
rise in blood

Figure 3.3. Type 2 diabetes is associated with insulin resistance, with an end result of increased blood glucose. The pancreas responds to the increased blood glucose by increasing insulin production. *Illustrator: Jeff Dixon.*

The mechanism of pathology of type 2 diabetes is very different from that of type 1 diabetes (see Figure 3.3). Type 2 diabetics are fully capable of producing sufficient amounts of insulin during the early stages of diagnosis. Although the exact mechanism has not yet been determined, it has been shown that the main problem of type 2 diabetics lies in the peripheral insulin receptors that have become resistant to the effects of insulin. Insulin is not able to bind to these receptors and is rendered useless in delivering sufficient amounts of glucose to the cells, causing glucose levels to rise in the blood. In addition to binding problems, other mechanisms can cause the same effects. These mechanisms include biochemical processes that occur after insulin has bound to the receptors on the cellular membrane. As a result, GLUT 4 receptors cannot travel to the cell membrane, and passage into the cytoplasm does not take place, causing glucose to back up into the bloodstream (Kahn 2007).

The resulting hyperglycemia sends signals back to the pancreas through a feedback loop to produce more insulin to compensate for the increased blood glucose. The pancreas works on feedback mechanisms that work to create a balance between glucose and energy conservation and utilization. Glucose is a major direct stimulator of the pancreatic beta cells, especially during hyperglycemia. These stimulatory effects of large amounts of glucose on the beta cells of the pancreas cause a release of large amounts of insulin. Despite the increased levels of insulin that are circulating, glucose remains in the bloodstream. There is a minor effect on sugar levels attributable to the primary condition of insulin resistance. Along with hyperglycemia, type 2 diabetics also present with hyperinsulinemia, which can provide clues to physicians during diagnosis. Regarding the feedback mechanisms, it can also be noticed that the inhibitory effects of insulin on the alpha cells are also present. Hyperinsulinemia causes a drastic inhibition on the alpha cells, causing a decline in glucagon levels (Pho 2005).

OBESE VS. NONOBESE TYPE 2 DIABETES

There are several categories that a type 2 diabetic can fall into that is determined by the weight of the patient. This classification is dependant on the body mass index (BMI). A BMI of less than 25 is considered to be a normal numerical proportion for a person's weight and height. A BMI within the range of 25–29.9 is considered overweight. Obesity is defined as a BMI that is greater that 30 and has gradations of obesity I, obesity II, and obesity III dependant on how elevated the BMI is (National Institutes of Health 2007). Type 2 diabetics can either be classified as obese or nonobese.

Obese type 2 diabetes is the most commonly diagnosed diabetes in the United States, comprising about 70 percent of diabetics. These patients have a BMI of over 30, placing them into the obese category. The mechanism of pathology in obese type 2 diabetes stems primarily from insensitivity to insulin, which leads to hyperglycemia. Patients present with a classic fat distribution primarily around their abdomen. Abdominal obesity, also referred to as an "apple shape," has been found to be a great risk factor for diabetes and heart disease (Rodriguez 1999). Along with this distribution of fat, obese patients have overnourished liver and muscles cells, which contribute to the decreased glucose uptake by those cells (Masharani, Karam, and German 2004).

Some patients can present with other biological manifestations in addition to hyperglycemia and obesity. A combination of hyperglycemia, increased insulin, dyslipidemia, and hypertension is known as metabolic syndrome, or syndrome X. The signs described by metabolic syndrome are a result of a chain of events that is stimulated by the initial hyperglycemia that was caused by insulin resistance. Increased levels of circulating insulin are a result of the positive stimulation of the pancreas by glucose. It has been shown that high insulin levels have an effect on the kidneys, causing an increased amount of salt retention. Increased salt levels in the bloodstream are linked with elevated blood pressure. Patients with metabolic syndrome are at a greater risk for developing associated diseases such as coronary artery disease and stroke attributable to the combined effects of poor glycemic control and hypertension. Physicians treating patients with metabolic syndrome must be aware of the combined effects of the risk factors and treat accordingly (Masharani, Karam, and German 2004).

Nonobese type 2 diabetes comprises about 30 percent of diabetics, presenting with a BMI of fewer than 29.9. The distribution of patients with the nonobese type varies depending on the genetic origin of the population. For example, a higher number of Asians are diagnosed with nonobese type, whereas Pacific Islanders and Pima Indians usually present with obese type 2 diabetes. The major defect in this group stems from a decreased amount of insulin secreted by the pancreatic beta cells along with a slight resistance to insulin by muscle, liver, and adipose cells. Despite the differences in pathological mechanisms of obese and nonobese patients, treatment regimens remain the same and are primarily aimed at proper glycemic control (Masharani, Karam, and German 2004).

The majority of type 2 diabetics are diagnosed with faulty glucose control after the age of forty, but certain patients can develop the disease before the age of twenty-five. Maturity-onset diabetes of the young (MODY) occurs in late childhood and is associated with a decreased response by the beta cells to glucose. MODY patients have been found to have a strong genetic correlation and family history of early-onset diabetes. There are six different classifications of MODY, each of which has specific associated genetic defects or mutations that are involved in glycemic control (Masharani, Karam, and German 2004).

PRESENTATION

Type 2 diabetics commonly present with symptoms similar to that of type 1 diabetics along with some differences. Commonalities between the two diseases include increased urination, thirst, blurred vision, and numbness attributable to the osmotic affects of increased circulating blood glucose. Because of the slow progression of the disease, many of these symptoms will not be felt until the hyperglycemia worsens. Usually, increased glucose levels are detected on routine medical blood tests along with urine dipsticks that test for the presence or absence of glucose. A common presenting symptom of type 2 diabetics is the presence of recurrent skin infections and poor wound healing. Women with type 2 diabetes usually present with similar infectious complaints along with vaginal colonization with *Candida* species. Men with type 2 diabetes will complain of impotence and sexual dysfunction as circulation to the sexual organs is decreased. One major difference between type 1 and type 2 diabetes is that type 2 diabetes patients are most commonly obese, with fat distribution centrally while the arms and legs are usually spared (Masharani, Karam, and German 2004).

Symptoms of diabetics usually present during the later stages of the disease along with complications. Patients can experience an increased thirst, increased urination, fatigue, blurred vision, dry and itchy skin, headache, and tingling of the extremities. Unmanaged diabetes results in blood vessel and nerve damage, which increases the susceptibility of diabetics to infections of the foot. Infections commonly go unnoticed because of decreased sensation caused by diabetic neuropathy, or nerve damage. A diabetic foot can progress to having a severe infection, which leads to tissue death. Damage to blood vessels is also responsible for the risk of infection because inadequate blood flow to the infected area leads to longer healing times. Death to certain parts of the foot caused by decreased circulation results in dry gangrene. Dry gangrene is associated with the risk of spreading to other parts of the body and must be contained. To prevent this spread, surgical intervention is required to amputate, or remove, a section of the foot that has developed gangrene. To prevent infections, diabetics are instructed to inspect their feet for open wounds or sores on a daily basis. In addition to foot infections, diabetics also experience more urinary tract infections, yeast infections, and skin infections than a healthy individual would. Slow healing times of cuts and bruises are also to common to diabetics because of decreased blood flow to the skin (Kahn 2007).

The symptoms of type 2 diabetics become apparent gradually, slowly progressing as the disease worsens. Blurry vision and foot pain are usually the first to be noticed and are early signs of progressive blood vessel and nerve damage. In comparison, type 1 diabetes has a faster onset of symptoms when pancreatic function ceases. Type 1 diabetes usually has a crisis point during which ketoacidosis attributable to severe hyperglycemia occurs. Type 2 diabetes, conversely, is usually suspected during routine blood tests that show abnormally high glucose levels. The silent onset of type 2 diabetic symptoms stresses the use of preventative measures to slow progression (Kahn 2007).

DIABETES IN PREGNANCY

One of the most common complications in pregnancy is diabetes. It includes a range of diseases, which can grossly be broken down into gestational and overt diabetes mellitus. Diabetes of pregnancy should be divided into gestational and pregestational diabetes, as opposed to nonpregnant diabetes, which is divided into type 1 and type 2. Gestational diabetes usually develops in the third trimester and is diagnosed by standard screening and diagnostic testing. If a pregnant woman is diagnosed with diabetes early in her pregnancy, one should consider that she might have undiagnosed pregestational diabetes. It is important to differentiate pregestational from gestational diabetes in pregnancy because each has different effects on both the mother and the baby.

True gestational diabetes mellitus (GDM) is "an impairment in carbohydrate metabolism that first manifests during pregnancy" (Callahan and Caughey 2006). It is recommended that all women be screened between weeks twenty-four and twenty-eight of pregnancy (Thompson 2005). One reason that diabetes may develop in pregnancy is that the placenta produces several hormones that have "anti-insulin" properties, for example, human placental lactogen. As the placenta increases in size, more of these hormones are produced, leading to more carbohydrate intolerance and insulin resistance. This is why diabetes does not usually present until later in the pregnancy. Although blood glucose levels usually return to normal after the pregnancy, these patients are at a fourfold to tenfold increased risk of developing overt diabetes mellitus later in life (Callahan and Caughey 2006).

Gestational diabetes is generally not life threatening to the mother but can cause problems for the growing fetus. Fetal macrosomia is a complication associated with GDM; fetal macrosomia means that the growing fetus is too large (more than 4,500 g). This can lead to failure of the baby to progress during labor or another serious birthing complication, shoulder distocia. This is where the shoulders of the baby are too broad to fit through the pelvis and the baby gets stuck. This can be dangerous for both the baby and the mother. In addition to this, the fetus is also at risk for neonatal hypoglycemia (from the high levels of sugar and insulin circulating in the bloodstream), as well as hypocalcemia, hyperbilirubinemia, and polycythemia, or the fetus may even die in the womb late in pregnancy, called fetal demise. These babies are also at risk in the future of developing childhood obesity and type 2 diabetes mellitus in early adulthood (Callahan and Caughey 2006).

The incidence of GDM ranges from 1 to 12 percent depending on the population. In the United States, there are higher rates of GDM among Hispanic, African American, and Native American women. In addition, there are increased rates seen in obese women, with advancing maternal age, with a family history, and with a previous infant weighing more than 4000 g. Women with risk factors should be screened. Some examples of risk factors include a family history of diabetes, especially in first-degree relatives, previous delivery of a baby greater than nine pounds, and age greater than twenty-five years. The American Diabetic Association also states that women at low risk may be omitted from screening, although it is common practice to screen all pregnant women (Jovanovic 2007).

As mentioned above, the best time to screen for GDM is at the end of the second trimester between weeks twenty-four and twenty-eight of pregnancy. Patients with one or more risk factor should be screened at their first prenatal visit and during each trimester. Screening for GDM generally consists of giving a load of 50 g of glucose and measuring the plasma glucose one hour later. If the one-hour glucose is above the screening threshold, then the screening test is positive, and a glucose tolerance test (GTT) must be performed. Recently, the screening threshold has been reduced from 140 mg/dl to between 130 and 135 mg/dl to increase the sensitivity.

If a woman's screening test is positive, she is then diagnosed with a three-hour GTT. This involves giving a 100 mg dose of oral glucose and measuring blood glucose levels before the dose is given and again at one, two, and three hours after the dose. A diagnosis is made if the fasting glucose or two or more of the after-meal glucose levels are elevated. Generally, a fasting blood glucose above 95 mg/dl, 180 mg/dl at one hour, 155 mg/dl at two hours, and 140 mg/dl at three hours is considered elevated.

A common classification used for diabetes during pregnancy is called the White Classification. For gestational diabetes, a pregnant woman who is diet controlled is termed A1, and a woman who needs additional medications is termed A2.

Usually when a woman is diagnosed with GDM, she is started on a diabetic diet (2,200 cal/day) with strict carbohydrate control and is instructed to do some light exercise each day, such as walking for fifteen minutes. If the diet plus exercise control the blood glucose, then it is continued throughout the pregnancy. If it does not control the blood glucose, oral hypoglycemics and/or insulin may be added for better control.

Pregnant women who develop GDM may be able to deliver normally if they are well controlled, but it is more common to deliver via scheduled induction at around thirty-nine weeks gestation. This is done to avoid a possible risk of hypoglycemia as the placenta begins to lose function. A woman who is poorly controlled will typically be delivered between thirty-seven and thirty-nine weeks once fetal lung maturity has been confirmed. Women who have an estimated fetal weight above 4,500 g are usually offered elective cesarean section.

Preexisting diabetes can have devastating effects on both the mother and the fetus during pregnancy. Women with pregestational diabetes are at risk for obstetrical complications, diabetic emergencies, vascular and end organ damage, and neurologic problems. In addition to these complications, diabetic pregnant women are also four times more likely to develop preeclampsia or eclampsia and are twice as likely to have a spontaneous abortion. There is also a fivefold increase in perinatal death and a twofold to threefold increase in congenital anomalies.

COMPLICATIONS

The hyperglycemic state that occurs in diabetes can result in serious long-term complications similar. Uncontrolled levels of blood glucose can eventually lead to heart disease, increased blood pressure, nerve damage, and kidney failure. These bodily states are dangerous and can affect other organs such as the eyes and even the lower extremities. Most of these long-term complications are preventable, assuming that the diabetic follows proper management protocol and controls blood glucose accordingly. Diet and exercise modifications are frequently used as the first line of defense in newly diagnosed patients. Weight control is the primary goal in diet therapy, and a reduced caloric intake is usually indicated for overweight individuals. Type 1 diabetics, conversely, modify the diet in relation to a delicate balance between carbohydrate intake and insulin therapy, not weight loss. In addition to diet, an exercise regimen is usually prescribed in conjunction with diet therapy in hopes to attain enhanced results.

A VISION IMPAIRED: THE DIABETIC EYE

Both type 1 and type 2 diabetics are at risk for developing a common complication known as diabetic retinopathy. Standard protocol in treatment and maintenance of diabetes indicates annual referrals and visits to a board-certified ophthalmologist. The ophthalmologist is a doctor that deals specifically with problems and diseases that relate to the eyes. Long-standing diabetes can have negative effects on the retina of the eye, often leading to blurred vision, floaters, and even loss of vision. Retinal changes occur after approximately twenty years of poorly controlled diabetes (Masharani, Karam, and German 2004).

The initial phase of retinopathy is known as the nonproliferative or background phase. This is caused by diabetic damage to the circulatory system and is the earliest manifestation of retinal pathology. Damage to arteries within the retina causes them to weaken and even rupture. The retina will display signs of pinpoint dot hemorrhages along with micro-aneurisms. Rupture of these capillary vessels causes fluids to leak out that contains proteins, lipids, and red blood cells. The collection of these substances within the retina causes swelling and edema, which causes a decline in the visual acuity of the diabetic's eye. Changes in visual function depend on the area of the retina that is affected and by the extent of the damage (Masharani, Karam, and German 2004).

The final stage of diabetic retinopathy is the result of the initial capillary blood vessel damage. As blood flow decreases as a result of rupture, less oxygen is able to reach the retina. This is known as ischemia, or oxygen deprivation. Decreased oxygen flow to the retina can be visualized as "cotton-wool" spots on examination of the eye. Blockage of blood to these areas stimulates the body to produce new blood vessels as a form of compensation. This is known as the process of neovascularization and is more commonly seen in type 1 diabetics approximately ten years after diagnosis. These newly formed blood vessels are not as strong as the previous ones and have the capability of rupturing under less strenuous conditions. Again, blood leaks into the retinal area, causing a decline in vision and an increase in floaters. Eventually, the constant creation and destruction of new blood vessels causes scar tissue to build up, which increases the risk for developing glaucoma or even retinal detachment. The series of events that take place during proliferative retinopathy is one of the leading causes of blindness in the United States. It is statistically shown that approximately 80 percent of diabetics develop some sort of retinopathy within fifteen years of having the disease (St. Lukes Cataract and Laser Institute 2007).

Prevention of diabetic retinopathy is the main goal of primary care physicians. This is achieved with the maintenance of proper blood glucose levels throughout the course of the disease. When complications occur, however, proper measures must be taken. Diagnosis of retinopathy can be attained by a combination of visual deficits along with positive findings on examination of the retina. On diagnosis, the progression of the disease and the severity determine treatment plans. The Diabetic Retinopathy Study was conducted and proved that surgical intervention with laser treatment is effective in controlling diabetic retinopathy. Surgery is performed using a laser with efforts to destroy ischemic retinal tissue. The destruction of this tissue halts growth of new vessels and simultaneously prevents leaks from reoccurring. Because parts of the retina are no longer functional after laser treatment, central parts remain viable and are able to receive a higher concentration of oxygenated blood (St. Lukes Cataract and Laser Institute 2007)

In addition to retinopathy, diabetics are at an increased risk for developing cataracts. Cataracts is an eye condition that is common to 50 percent of people over the age of sixty-five and increases in frequency as one gets older. The normal eye has a lens that is involved in focusing light onto the retina. The lens in a healthy individual is clear and passes light without any interference. A cataract signifies a lens that has become cloudy, preventing light from being bent in the proper direction. A cataract causes vision to become blurry or hazy along with a dulled color perspective (National Eye Institute 2006). Patients with cataracts will initially complain of difficulty reading or driving at night. Type 1 diabetics are prone to developing a certain type of cataract known as subcapsular, which is exacerbated by conditions of hyperglycemia. Subcapsular cataracts affect the posterior portion of the lens and have a faster time of onset than other forms of cataracts. Nuclear cataracts are considered to be age related. Uncontrolled diabetics are at a greater risk of developing nuclear cataracts at an earlier age than those without underlying hyperglycemia (Masharani, Karam, and German 2004).

There are two mechanisms that are involved in the development of cataracts that are directly linked to diabetes. The first mechanism involved is directly linked to long-standing hyperglycemia. Various proteins that are found on the lens of the eye are subjected to increased levels of sugars. These sugars are actually linked and added to structural proteins and lipids of the lens, which contributes to clouding. The process of sugars binding to proteins or lipids is known as glycosylation. The second mechanism involved is attributable to increased levels of sorbitol that is found on the lens because of hyperglycemia. Glucose that is found in the eye is slowly converted to sorbitol, which collects in high concentrations in the lens. The high sorbitol levels cause increased amounts of water to be shifted into the lens, which causes a disfiguration. The osmotic pressure of the water causes a change in lens shape that eventually leads to damage of the lens and cataract formation. The combination of both glycosylation and elevated sorbitol levels leads to the formation of cataracts in diabetics at a faster rate than those without the disease. Proper control of blood sugars through medications should help to decrease the effects of diabetes on the lens of the eye (Kinshuck 2007).

Diabetics with long-standing cataracts eventually develop vision problems that are incompatible with daily life and may need surgical correction. Cataract surgery is a relatively safe procedure with a 95 percent success rate. Implications for surgery vary on an individual basis according to the needs of the patient and by their visual needs. The eye surgeon begins the operation by inserting a small probe into the lens of the eye and taking out the clouded portion of the cataracts. After removal of this material, a properly measured artificial lens is implanted in its place. The procedure is fairly quick and without complications, and the patient can leave the hospital after several hours.

Within two to seven days after surgery, normal daily activities can be resumed. Because diabetic cataracts usually affect both eyes simultaneously, both eyes are operated on but on two separate occasions two weeks apart (Kinshuck 2007).

KIDNEYS IN A CRISIS

The kidneys are involved in filtering out toxins from the bloodstream into the urine. The kidneys play an important role in maintaining a proper balance of protein and electrolytes in the blood. This filtration system should function properly in healthy individuals; however, diabetics are susceptible to loss of kidney function. Both type 1 and type 2 diabetics are susceptible to a decline in kidney function with long-standing disease (see Figure 3.4). Type 1 diabetics are twice as likely to develop renal failure when compared with type 2 diabetics. Kidney failure or nephropathy occurs after fifteen to twenty years of ongoing uncontrolled diabetes. Diabetes causes one-third of all renal failure in

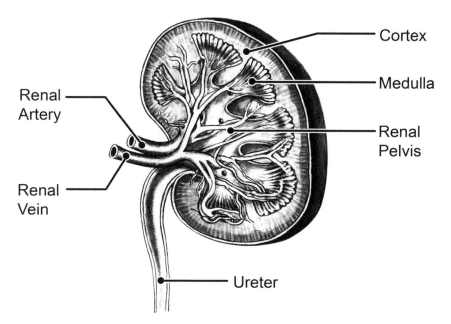

Figure 3.4. The renal artery supplies blood to the kidney. The functional unit of the kidney is the nephron, which is found in the renal cortex and the renal medulla. Urine from the kidneys travels into the renal pelvis to eventually reach the ureter. *Illustration courtesy of Michael Brookman.*

the United States and increases in frequency as the duration of the disease progresses (Masharani, Karam, and German 2004).

The high sugar content in the blood of diabetics takes its toll on the kidneys. Normally, the nephrons of the kidney filter out toxins, whereas larger molecules such as proteins and red blood cells are left back in the circulation. The first manifestation of renal demise is the presence of small concentrations of protein within the urine. The most frequently tested for protein is serum albumin. Albumin is produced by the liver and accounts for a large percentage of protein within the blood. Albumin plays a large role in maintaining osmotic forces within the blood. Physicians commonly use urine dipsticks to measure albumin concentrations in the urine. A positive finding of albumin is labeled as microalbuminuria and is suggestive of kidney pathology. A more specific test would be an overnight urine collection that measures albumin levels in the first urine specimen on awakening. A value that is greater than 20 μg of albumin per liter of urine on three separate occasions is considered to be diagnostic for microalbuminuria (Omachi 1986).

Findings of minute amounts of albumin in the urine are associated with increased blood pressure, which is another risk factor for kidney damage along with vascular problems. A biopsy of the kidneys will reveal a thickening of the membrane of the nephron. As time progresses, a greater number of nephrons are destroyed and kidney function declines (Kimmelstiel and Wilson 1936). Fluid retention causes an increase in the volume of blood within the arteries and veins, causing increased blood pressure and edema. Patients initially will not experience any symptoms, but, as disease progresses, they will begin to experience swelling of the orbits of the eyes and ankles along with weight gain from excess water retention (Masharani, Karam, and German 2004).

Nephropathy is prevented by controlling glucose levels properly by adhering to treatment plans set forth by a physician. Early treatment is usually through oral glycemic agents or insulin therapy with goals to achieve proper glycemic control. Along with strict management of blood glucose levels, other pharmacological methods can be used to control renal manifestations as well. On diagnosis of protein in the urine, the mainstay treatment is an angiotensin converting enzyme (ACE) inhibitor. ACE inhibitors are used as agents to normalize blood pressure but are used in diabetic patients to decrease the progression of diabetic nephropathy. ACE inhibitors have been clinically proven to reduce the amount of protein that is excreted in the urine and to decrease the risk of progression of kidney failure (Masharani, Karam, and German 2004).

Progressive diabetic nephropathy is associated with an increase in blood pressure along with edema, which is a collection of fluids throughout certain areas of the body. The presence of progressive diabetic nephropathy is associated with an increased risk for developing atherosclerosis. In this stage of the disease, glycemic control alone is not sufficient enough to prevent progression. Blood pressure-lowering medications, ACE inhibitors, and protein restriction are the mainstay treatments (Masharani, Karam, and German 2004).

If treatment is unsuccessful or ineffective, the kidneys eventually lose their function and the patient will require dialysis or a kidney transplant. Dialysis is a treatment given to patients with end-stage renal disease who cannot properly excrete toxins from their system. To prevent the buildup of such materials, a hemodialysis machine can be used to artificially filter the blood. The blood of the patient is sent into the machine and is exposed to various filters and membranes that replicate the function of the nephron. After passage of the blood through this machine, it is sent back into the systemic circulation free of toxins. The average patient must be treated with hemodialysis three times a week for three-hour intervals. Another type of dialysis is peritoneal dialysis, which is more convenient and has less associated risk. In peritoneal dialysis, a solution is pumped into the abdominal cavity and osmotic forces act to filter out waste materials through the peritoneal membrane. After a period of time, the solution along with the filtered substances are collected and removed from the peritoneal cavity. Although this process is less efficient than hemodialysis, it is growing in popularity because it can be done at one's home and does not require frequent visits to a dialysis center.

Another option for treating end-stage renal disease is a kidney transplant. In a transplant, a nonfunctioning kidney is replaced by a functioning kidney that is taken from either a living or a deceased person. Kidneys that are transplanted must be screened for compatibility before the procedure to minimize the risk of rejection by the receiver's immune system. Surgery takes about three hours to complete, and the patient must take immunosuppressive medications to have successful results. Transplant patients have been shown to have a 94 percent survival rate within the first year of treatment and an 80 percent survival rate within five years of receiving treatment. Despite the success rates of kidney transplantation, it is often difficult to find compatible donors, and waiting lists for kidney transplants can take years (Barry 2002).

MAKING SENSE OF THE NERVES

One of the most commonly experienced complications of diabetes is a neurological pathology known as a neuropathy. Although the development of neuropathy and the link between the diabetic condition is poorly understood, it is hypothesized that it can be attributable to either decreased oxygen flow to the nerve cells or damage from osmotic forces. Under the effects of long-standing diabetes, hyperglycemia takes its toll on the nerves. One way in which this happens is when there is a decreased flow of blood to a neuron. Decreased blood flow to an area causes ischemic changes in which oxygen flow is lowered substantially. Osmotic forces also cause changes in cellular mechanisms that can lead to faulty signal conduction (Masharani, Karam, and German 2004).

Neuropathy can either be peripheral or autonomic. The peripheral nervous system consists of nerves that innervate organs that are under voluntary control such as skeletal muscle, along with sensory signals from the periphery that deal with vibration, pain, and temperature. Diabetics usually have defective conduction of sensory information and diminished or absent deep tendon reflexes. Usually sensory deficits occur bilaterally and symmetrically. A reflex hammer can be used to check the status of deep tendon reflexes. In a normal knee-jerk reflex, the patients legs are allowed to hang freely off of the examination table. The patellar tendon, found just below the knee, is quickly hit with a reflex hammer, causing the leg on the same side to extend and swing forward to compensate for the stretched tendon. Reflexes are rated on a scale of 0 to 5, in which 0 signifies an absent reflex and 5 signifies a very intense and sustained knee jerk. A simple test can be performed to check the status of vibratory sensation as well by using a tuning fork. The tuning fork is hit and placed on a bony prominence near the ankle joint. The doctor will ask the patient if vibration is felt and for how long. A decreased or absent vibratory sense can be warning signs for more serious neurological conditions to occur if the condition goes untreated. The most significant sensory deficit that a diabetic can experience is that of pain. Pain sensation is drastically decreased in nerves that pass through canals such as in the ankle. An absent pain sensation, particularly in the foot, puts diabetics at risk for developing foot ulcers without realization of the damage taking place (Masharani, Karam, and German 2004).

In addition to the sensory losses, diabetics can sometimes develop paralysis of skeletal muscles. This paralysis is caused by nerve damage that stems from an occluded artery. Decreased blood flow to a certain area destroys nerves, causing paralysis along with atrophy of the affected muscle group. Diagnosis of motor neuropathies is based on focal lesions that are found and neurological signs. For example, a lesion of the facial nerve, cranial nerve seven, will result in facial paralysis (Masharani, Karam, and German 2004).

Treatment for peripheral neuropathy is usually with good glycemic control and amitriptyline, which helps to reduce discomfort of lower leg pain. If this treatment regimen is not sufficient to relieve pain, a stronger pharmacologic treatment of gabapentin can be used. It is also important to show the diabetic patient how to properly care for their feet and frequently visit a foot care specialist (Masharani, Karam, and German 2004).

The high level of sugar in the blood has toxic effects on organs in the body. Studies have shown that high blood sugar states can cause permanent organ damage and cause further diabetic states. The GTT is a diagnostic tool used by doctors to measure how effectively an individual's body handles a measured dose of glucose. Blood tests are taken several hours later to measure the level of glucose in the bloodstream. Researchers at the University of Utah found that patients that had a high GTT (140 mg/dg after a two-hour reading) experienced a sensation of tingling and burning in their extremities. These sensations are caused by peripheral neuropathy or nerve damage, showing the toxic effects that hyperglycemia can produce. A similar study conducted at Johns Hopkins University found that patients that experienced nerve pain for unknown reasons had abnormal GTTs. Patients with GTTs at levels of diabetics were found to have large nerve involvement

The autonomic nervous system is responsible for the involuntary actions of the body such as breathing, digestion, and heart rate. Each organ can be affected, causing specific constitutional symptoms. The digestive tract is commonly affected in autonomic neuropathy. This results in varied effects of gastric motility, usually presenting as diarrhea or constipation along with vomiting, nausea, and gastric reflux. Alterations in gastric motility can lead to varied peaks and troughs of blood glucose levels and should be checked using radiographic studies. Diabetic diarrhea also presents with an increased risk for bacterial infections that can be treated with antibiotics (Masharani, Karam, and German 2004).

In addition to gastrointestinal problems, circulatory problems such as orthostatic hypotension can also result from autonomic neuropathy. Orthostatic hypertension is defined as a drop in blood pressure by either 20 mmHg systolically or 10 mmHg diastolically when rising from a sitting position to a standing position. This sudden drop in blood pressure causes a feeling of dizziness, lightheadedness, and even temporary visual disturbances. Diabetics that experience these symptoms should be placed on medications to prevent such occurrences and to reduce the risk of falls. There are several ways to reduce orthostatic hypotension. One way is to wear Jobst stockings, which provide a compressive force to the lower extremities and prevent excess blood from pooling in the veins. This allows more blood to remain within the circulation and keeps blood pressure levels within normal limits. Patients are sometimes advised to increase their salt intake slightly with the intent to raise their blood pressure.

Impotence is also a feature that is common to diabetics experiencing autonomic neuropathy. Impotence is the inability to achieve an erection and is also known as erectile dysfunction. It has been estimated that approximately

75 percent of diabetics will experience some form of erectile dysfunction. Diabetic men develop erectile dysfunction ten years earlier than those men without the disease (Masharani, Karam, and German 2004). Autonomic neuropathy affects those nerves that are responsible for sending signals to the penile tissue to become erect. Erectile dysfunction in a diabetic is usually constant, and nocturnal erections do not occur compared with other forms. Sildenafil has been shown to help with diabetic neuropathies in regards to impotence. Similar mechanisms of neuropathy also have an affect on urination secondary to loss of bladder control. Bladder weakness can also present, in which the patient complains of difficulty voiding because of a poor or absent bladder tone. Patients that present with these signs should be treated with medications that will improve bladder tone to decrease the risk of urinary stasis and infection (Baird 2007).

A VESSEL OF CARDIAC COMPLICATIONS

Diabetics are at an increased risk for developing cardiovascular complications, including coronary heart disease, stroke, peripheral arterial disease, nephropathy, retinopathy, and possibly neuropathy and cardiomyopathy. Diabetes is now considered to be a cardiovascular disease. Both type 1 and type 2 diabetes are considered to be risk factors for developing coronary heart disease, and atherosclerosis is commonly found on examination of the vasculature (Grundy et al. 1999).

Atherosclerosis affects the arteries of the circulatory system. Arteries are involved in carrying blood away from the heart toward the direction of the body and peripheral organs. A normal artery is elastic and resilient and can stretch to accommodate blood flow. Atherosclerosis is the result of slow deposition of substances such as lipoproteins, which form deposits known as plaques on the walls of the artery. As these plaques accumulate, the arteries lose their elasticity and become hardened and less resilient to changes in shape. As this process progresses, less blood is able to pass through the vasculature, causing a decreased blood flow to the tissue that is being supplied. Diabetics commonly present with atherosclerosis and do not display symptoms of the disease. The lack of symptoms along with late medical attention leads to a decreased survival rate for diabetics. Because of these outcomes, having diabetes is considered to be the equivalent to atherosclerosis (Bhatt and Topol 2002).

Diabetics are three times more likely to experience a fatal stroke than those without disease. Stroke is the number three cause of death in the United States. A stroke occurs when blood flow to the brain is compromised by either an obstruction or the rupture of a vessel, thereby preventing oxygen and nutrients from reaching cells. This obstruction leads to death of brain tissue and leads to outcomes dependant on the area that was injured. In diabetes, high blood sugars in the systemic circulation cause damage to the blood vessels. The atherosclerotic plaques that result from this damage build up and become susceptible, breaking off the vessel wall and traveling into the systemic circulation. The plaques that deposit on the carotid arteries pose a great risk for dislodging and traveling into the vasculature of the brain, thereby causing a stroke. About 13 percent of diabetics that are over the age of sixty-five have suffered from a stroke (Masharani, Karam, and German 2004).

Diabetics are at a great risk for developing heart problems without knowledge of their existence. According to the results of the Detection of Silent Myocardial Ischemia in Asymptomatic Diabetic Subjects, 20 percent of patients with asymptomatic diabetes have silent myocardial ischemia. These findings support the American Diabetes Association (ADA) guidelines recommending routine screening. According to Dr. Richard Shloftmitz, director of the Cardiac Catheterization Laboratory at St. Francis Hospital, "diabetes is actually clinically a vascular disease involving all blood vessels from the brain, eyes, heart, kidneys and legs. Therefore all diabetic patients should have routine vascular screening from head to toe, especially since the neuropathy that they frequently experience might not warn them early in the disease since they wouldn't have symptoms." Dr. Shlofmitz states that "CT [computed tomography] angiography is an excellent screening examination for diabetic patients. Since diabetic patients are at high risk for cardiac events, aggressive preventive medicine is critical in this group. CTA [computed tomography angiography] is one of the most effective noninvasive assessments especially in asymptomatic patients. Recommendations in this group of patients for early detection would be across the board unless the patient had renal insufficiency or contraindications to contrast agent."

The onset of diabetic cardiomyopathy is faster in diabetic patients when compared with those without the disease. Cardiomyopathy is a disease of the heart in which the cardiac muscles are weak and cannot efficiently pump blood throughout the systemic circulation. The accelerated onset of cardiomyopathy in diabetics is attributable to the associated coronary atherosclerosis, prolonged hypertension, chronic hyperglycemia, microvascular disease, glycosylation of myocardial proteins, and autonomic neuropathy. Each factor can be attended to individually to prevent further development of cardiomyopathy. One way is to control blood glucose levels within a strict range along with antihypertensive agents such as ACE inhibitors and cholesterol-lowering drugs (Grundy et al. 1999).

Myocardial infarction is found to be five times more common in diabetic patients when compared when individuals of the same age without the disease.

Also known as a heart attack, a myocardial infarction results when there is a cessation of blood flow to certain areas of the heart. Deceased blood flow results in a decrease in oxygen availability, causing damage and even death to the tissues that are affected. Diabetes is considered to be an independent risk factor along with tobacco use, obesity, high blood pressure, and old age. Prevention of risk factors is the most important method to decrease the chances of having a heart attack, such as smoking cessation and control of blood pressure and diabetes. The Heart Outcomes Prevention Evaluation Study found that placing diabetics on an ACE inhibitor decreased the risk of developing a cardiovascular incident by 25 percent. Along with an ACE inhibitor, a dose of 81 mg of aspirin daily is recommended by the ADA to prevent vascular manifestations (Masharani, Karam, and German 2004).

In addition to the toxic effects that glucose has on the nervous system, it is now known that hyperglycemia causes beta cell failure. Long-term damage to these cells produces a decrease in insulin secretion, contrary to the early stages of diabetes, which displayed hyperinsulinemia. Individuals with pancreatic failure are not able to produce insulin and, like type 1 diabetics, become dependant on supportive insulin therapy. The San Antonio Metabolism Study found that high results of the oral glucose test correlated to pancreatic beta cell failure (Gastaldelli et al. 2004). Another study, led by Butler, autopsied deceased patients who were known to have glucose tests near the upper limit of normal (Butler et al. 2003). During autopsy, the researchers discovered that these patients lost approximately 40 percent of their pancreatic beta cells. Taking this experiment to the cellular level, researcher Paul Robertson exposed culture-grown beta cells to high blood sugar. The results of the experiment showed irreversible damage to the beta cells. Modifying this experiment, researchers were able to find the threshold exposure time needed to elapse before cell death occurs.

Hyperglycemia has been found to damage cells even at lower blood sugars. The term pre-diabetes was developed to categorize individuals with blood glucose levels within the upper limits of normal, just below that of a diabetic diagnosis. These individuals were found to be at risk for diabetic retinopathy, despite not being diagnosed with diabetes. Pre-diabetes poses a potential threat to cardiovascular heart as well. A study presented to the American Heart Association in 2006 showed a linear correlation with blood sugars in the pre-diabetic range and occurrence of heart failure.

KETOACIDOSIS

In addition to developing high levels of glucose within the bloodstream, type 1 diabetics are at a high risk for developing ketoacidosis. Ketoacidosis occurs when high levels of ketones are released from the breakdown products of muscle and fat cells. The pH of the bloodstream is dramatically lowered with the accumulation of these ketones and can be dangerous to the body. Type 1 diabetics with ketoacidosis may experience physical warning signs, including dry skin, vomiting, difficulty breathing, and confusion. High concentrations of ketones within the bloodstream can be toxic and can even lead to diabetic coma. High levels of ketones are easily tested for using specialized urine strips that test for ketone bodies. Ketoacidosis is a warning sign that an individual's diabetes is out of control, and patients usually find themselves admitted to a hospital after such an occurrence.

WATCH YOUR STEP: THE DIABETIC FOOT

Diabetics are prone to foot problems because of the combination of vascular and neurological problems that result from long-standing hyperglycemia. Approximately 15 percent of patients with diabetes develop foot ulcers (see Figure 3.5). Through self checks and frequent visits to a physician, many of these complications can be prevented if detected early. Many foot conditions can result from diabetes, ranging in severity including infections, calluses, bunions, and ulcers. Widespread infections can even result in the need to amputate a portion of the foot that is affected (McCulloch 2007a).

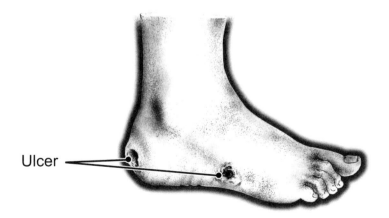

Ulcer

Figure 3.5. Diabetics with neurological and circulatory problems are prone to the development of foot ulcers. Patients are instructed to keep feet clean and to perform daily foot checks to prevent the formation of these sores. *Illustration courtesy of Michael Brookman.*

All patients with diabetes should be educated on the importance of basic foot care that should be performed daily along with regular visits to physicians and foot care specialists known as podiatrists. In addition to tightly controlling blood glucose levels, daily inspection and care of a diabetic's foot will increase the chances of early detection of possible problems. Diabetics are instructed to wash their feet daily with warm water and soap. Application of a moisturizing lotion is also beneficial. Cutting toenails with scissors or clippers by the patient should be avoided; rather, a nail file should be used to eliminate sharp edges. A podiatrist should manage ingrown toenails and blisters. Stress is placed on proper footwear that is properly fitted and is not too tight. Clean and properly fitted cotton socks are also recommended to be worn with and without shoes because walking barefoot can increase the chances of causing further damage. A orthotic insole can also be used to decrease loads on weight-bearing areas of the foot. It is important to avoid activities that can damage the feet as well, such as walking barefoot and exposure to hot temperatures (such as a heating pad and hot baths; McCulloch 2006).

Diabetics with long-standing hyperglycemia have an increased risk of damaging blood vessels and nerves that are responsible for maintaining the integrity of the foot. Approximately 80 percent of patients with foot ulcers have an associated neuropathy that is responsible for the ulcer formation. Neuropathy is present in 50 percent of patients that are over the age of sixty years and is a contributing risk factor for the development of foot ulcers. Ulcer formation can go unnoticed by the patient because of decreased sensation of pain and pressure on contact. An unnoticed lesion at a pressure spot can progress to pathological condition if not cared for properly (McCulloch 2006). It is therefore important for diabetics to visually inspect their lower extremities on a daily basis as a preventative measure. Ulcers that are not prevented can be difficult to treat because of a decreased circulation to the affected lesions (McCulloch 2007a).

Untreated diabetes and foot ulcers can increase the risk of serious infections, resulting in gangrene and necessitating amputation of a portion of the foot. Gangrene results when the tissues of the foot die and begin to decay. Prevention of foot amputation is possible through early intervention by both the patient and the treating physician (McCulloch 2007a). When infection is diagnosed, the patient is instructed to clean the wound and replace dressings regularly. In addition to cleaning, antibiotics are prescribed to assist the body with eliminating the infectious agent. The treatment of ulcers should be followed by a physician on a weekly basis to monitor progress. A complicated infection may require an admission to a hospital for more intense testing and treatment. Treatment at a hospital includes intravenous antibiotics and possibly surgery (McCulloch 2006).

Diabetes is a complex disease that encompasses many aspects of physiology. The pathology of type 1 diabetes differs from that of type 2 as discussed above. Many of the complications of diabetes are severe and have an affect on numerous organ systems. These complications can be prevented with success-ful management of diabetes through life modifications and drug therapies. In the following chapter, we will discuss how diabetes is diagnosed and treated through various means.

4

Testing and Treatment

DETECTIVE WORK

Because of the importance of detecting diabetes as quickly as possible, testing has always been a vital component of diabetes research and treatment. Throughout the years, there has been an ongoing evolution in blood testing that allows for increasingly precise diagnosis of diabetes based on sugar levels. Early testing and monitoring of blood glucose levels plays an important role in patients presenting with risk factors or symptoms, and early detection is an integral part in the prevention of complications caused by this disease process.

Despite the ongoing research in preventative management of diabetes, today's medicinal knowledge relies heavily on blood tests to make a firm diagnosis of type 1 diabetes. The most common blood test performed is the plasma glucose test. This test is the preferred test in establishing a diagnosis and is considered to be the most accurate gauge of diabetic status. The plasma glucose test requires an eight-hour fasting period, during which the individual is restricted from eating or drinking with the exception of water. The reason for fasting is to allow the body's insulin to distribute glucose into peripheral cells without loading it with additional glucose. After the fasting period, a blood sample is taken and glucose levels are measured. A healthy person would commonly have a glucose level that ranges from 70 to 100 mg/dl. Results greater than 126 mg/dl label the patient as hyperglycemic, meaning that the person is diabetic (Kahn 2007).

In addition to the plasma glucose test, other tests such as the random glucose test and oral GTT can be used for individuals that present with diabetic symptoms. The random glucose test, unlike the plasma glucose test, does not require a fasting period and is so named because it can be taken randomly at any time of the day. Once again, blood is drawn and analyzed for glucose content. A glucose reading of more than 200 mg/dl is considered a positive marker for diabetes. The oral GTT is used to measure how efficiently the body adjusts to a specific quantity of ingested glucose over a set period of time. The patient is instructed to drink a mixture containing exactly 75 g of glucose. After ingestion, blood samples are taken at specific time intervals to measure the effectiveness of glucose metabolism and uptake. Blood taken two hours after drinking the glucose mixture is examined for its glucose content. Results over 200 mg/dl provide physicians with enough evidence of faulty glucose metabolism to produce a diagnosis of diabetes (Kahn 2007).

There are many tests that can be performed to check for the presence of type 1A diabetes. Most of these procedures test for antibodies that can be found in the bloodstream. Antibodies are proteins that are made by the immune system in response to foreign particles that enter the body. These antibodies are used to remove antigens from the organism with great specificity. In the case of type 1A diabetes, antibodies are formed against certain molecular compounds related to the pancreas and insulin production. For example, antibodies against islet cells found in blood samples are suggestive of autoimmune, or type 1A, diabetes. Other tests include anti-GAD and anti-insulin antibodies. Positive test results for these molecules can help to establish a diagnosis of the type 1A subtype (Powers 2004).

Diagnosis of type 2 diabetes is based on the principal of hyperglycemia. Both type 1 and type 2 diabetes share the same characteristic of high blood sugar and are thus diagnosed in similar manners. Tests for type 2 diabetes include fasting plasma glucose test, random plasma glucose, and oral GTT. Positive results for these tests must be checked again on a subsequent basis to confirm the diagnosis of type 2 diabetes with certainty. In some clinical presentations, it may be difficult to differentiate between type 1 and type 2 diabetes using only physical findings and blood glucose tests. In this case, the C-peptide test, which measures levels of a certain protein that is linked with insulin production, can be used. Because type 1 diabetics lack insulin-producing beta cells, levels of C-peptide in the blood will be very low to nonexistent. In addition to distinguishing the type of diabetes present, the

C-peptide test can be used to monitor beta cell activity in type 2 diabetics who are at risk for pancreatic failure. Other tests include the islet cell antibody test, anti-insulin test, and anti-GAD test. Positive results for these tests dismiss a type 2 diagnosis, proving that an autoimmune process is taking place (Kahn 2007).

During the diagnostic process, other tests should be performed to create baseline figures, with which one can quantify the effectiveness of treatment. These tests include a reading of hemoglobin A1C levels along with cholesterol levels and an electrocardiogram. Obtaining these results allows physicians to determine the aggressiveness of treatment along with modifications in drug regimens.

TREATMENT OPTIONS

Treatment of diabetes is aimed at controlling the glucose levels to prevent further complications of the disease. Diabetic therapy involves proper guidance from a physician to establish a regimen for the patient. Each regimen is dependant on the type of diabetes, status and progression of symptoms, along with associated diseases embodied in the patient in question. Because diabetes is a chronic disease that is present throughout one's life, treatment must be pursued indefinitely and must conform to the patient's lifestyle. Initial treatment of diabetes consists of prescribing the patient a proper nutritional diet along with an exercise regimen to reverse glycemic effects. Secondary treatment consists of oral anti-diabetic drugs that work with various mechanisms to control glucose and insulin levels of the blood. Insulin treatment is also given by injection to diabetics who cannot produce viable levels of insulin on their own. Monitoring blood glucose levels, an important feature in the management of diabetes, is done using portable glucose meters. In addition to lifestyle changes and pharmacological supplements, frequent visits to a physician are necessary to track the progression of the disease to alter levels of medications and keep treatments on a positive course.

It is important for type 2 diabetics to control their blood glucose levels to prevent harmful consequences of hyperglycemia. One way for diabetics to manage their levels is through careful alteration of eating habits and diet modifications. Type 2 diabetics must conform to a well-defined schedule or pattern of eating. Working together with a physician, diabetics are assigned a proper diet containing specific amount of fats, proteins, and carbohydrates to be ingested on a daily basis. A registered dietician can also be helpful in establishing a proper regimen. The goal of a diabetes diet regimen is to coordinate caloric intake with insulin administration in hopes of maintaining blood glucose levels near normal. "When you're talking about diabetes, there is no 'one size fits all' diet," said Ann Albright of the ADA. "For people with diabetes and those at risk for type 2 diabetes, medical nutrition therapy should be tailored to a person's specific health issues and personal preferences to help maintain optimum health by controlling blood glucose levels, blood pressure, cholesterol, and other risk factors. We hope these recommendations will help people make better choices about what they eat and how they live to maximize their chances of staying healthy" (Morgan 2006). This is done by looking at the glycemic index, which measures the effects of certain types of carbohydrates in blood sugar. By sustaining proper levels of blood sugar, diabetics are protected against heart and kidney complications that are common in unmanaged diabetics (Morgan 2006).

A TASTY SOLUTION

Annually, the ADA releases a diabetic food pyramid. This should be used as the mainstay diet of diabetics. Daily caloric allowances are within the range of 1,600–2,800 calories depending on one's physical demands and lifestyle. When compared with the traditional food pyramid that is recommended by the U.S. Department of Agriculture (USDA), the ADA food pyramid is categorized by carbohydrate and protein content rather than food type. Carbohydrates are grouped together and include carbohydrates from fruits, vegetables, whole grains, legumes, and low-fat milk. Serving sizes have been modified to make carbohydrate content about the same in each serving. When a caloric goal has been established, it is important to divide the total amount into a series of meals and snacks throughout the day.

The ADA recommends six to eleven servings of carbohydrates per day. Serving sizes for foods containing carbohydrates have been compared with ingesting one slice of bread. For example, one-third cup of rice is considered to be the equivalent in carbohydrates as eating one slice of bread and is therefore one serving. Vegetables that contain starch such as potatoes and yam are grouped in the carbohydrate category. Three to five servings of noncarbohydrate vegetables are recommended daily. These vegetables contain numerous vitamins and minerals that are high in fiber and low in fat. Such vegetables include chicory, sorrel, Swiss chard, broccoli, cabbage, bok Choy, Brussels sprouts, cauliflower, kale, carrots, tomatoes, cucumbers, and lettuce (Warshaw 1996). Fruits contain carbohydrates along with vitamins and fiber. It is recommended that diabetics eat two to four servings of fruit daily, including blackberries, cantaloupe, strawberries, oranges, apples, bananas, peaches, pears, apricots, and grapes (Warshaw 1996). Similar quantification of serving sizes was done for dairy products as well as meats. According to the ADA website, diabetics should "choose from lean meats, poultry and fish and cut all the visible fat off meat ... [keeping] portion sizes small. Three ounces is about the size of a deck of cards ... 4–6 ounces [is recommended] for the whole day" (American Diabetes Association 2005a). Patients can manage their meals throughout the day with these recommendations.

Newly diagnosed diabetics may find it difficult to maintain a proper diet, but the Diabetes Food Pyramid simplifies the process, thereby increasing the chances of maintaining proper nutrition. Physicians usually refer diabetics for a nutritional consult with a registered dietician for a more detailed explanation of the diabetic diet.

FITTING ACTIVITIES

Along with diet, exercise habits must also be accounted for in the management of a diabetic patient. Any changes in these daily scheduled patterns can result in poorly controlled blood glucose levels, leading to devastating side effects. Exercise consists of any type of physical activity that stimulates the body to function above baseline for a given period of time. The recommended time for physical activity for people with diabetes is for "at least 30 minutes on five or more days of the week" (American Diabetes Association n.d.). Exercise includes a wide variety of physical activities that can be molded to the patient's lifestyle and abilities ranging from walking and swimming to dancing. The regimen that a physician prescribes to a patient encompasses the current health of the individual to determine the level of physical activity that can be safely performed.

Physical activity is a first-line treatment for newly diagnosed diabetics because of the beneficial physiological changes that occur. Exercise helps to lower blood glucose, blood pressure, and cholesterol. Along with these lowering effects, studies have found that exercise can reduce the risk of cardiovascular problems by improving circulation and enhances the function of insulin within the body (American Diabetes Association n.d.). Weight loss is also beneficial for type 2 diabetics who are prone to obesity. Weight loss relieves excess strains on the body and increases range of motion and function.

Despite the benefits of physical activity, caution must be taken to control blood glucose levels to prevent hypoglycemia. It is important to check blood glucose levels before exercising and compensate for a potentially drastic drop especially in type 1 diabetics who are being treated with insulin. Hypoglycemia can be prevented by ingesting small snacks or glucose tablets and by properly timing insulin injections to correlate with exercise.

Many times, compliance with diet and exercise regimens can become ineffective, and other interventions must be considered. Through close observation of hemoglobin A1C levels, a physician can determine whether the administration of pharmaceutical treatment is necessary. Hemoglobin A1C offers a way to monitor long-term glycemic control in patients over a three-month period of time. The goal of treatment is to maintain A1C levels that are under 7; this can be achieved with greater success through a combination of lifestyle changes along with medications (McCulloch 2007b).

TODAY'S TABLETS

A persistent state of hyperglycemia that does not remit with diet and exercise calls for monotherapy with metformin. Metformin belongs to a group of medications known as biguanides and is useful in the treatment of sustained hyperglycemia because it helps to reduce blood glucose. There is a noticeable decline in levels of fasting blood glucose along with a decrease in the amount of hyperglycemia after the ingestion of a meal. Metformin does not directly stimulate the pancreas to produce insulin like other diabetes medications, but it does alter the action of the insulin that is secreted. Although the exact mechanism of action of the drug is not yet known, it is believed that metformin's therapeutic effects are on the liver as well as skeletal muscles in the periphery. Within the liver, metformin decreases the amount of glucose that is produced and released into the bloodstream. The skeletal muscles increase the amount of glucose that they uptake from the circulation. In addition to these benefits, metformin has also been found to aid in weight reduction by decreasing appetite, a significant benefit for type 2 diabetes that have a underlying obesity. The overall effect is a total decline in glucose levels and an increase of glucose absorption into the cells that need it (Masharani, Karam, and German 2004).

Metformin is an oral medication in the form of a tablet that comes in doses of 500 and 850 mg. Patients are usually started on a low dose that is gradually increased over time. A usual regimen begins with the administration of one 500 mg tablet, taken with a meal, in the evening. Close observation of glycemic levels by a physician and monitoring the side effects, another 500 mg tablet can be added to the regimen that is taken with a morning meal. The maximum effective dose consists of 850 mg tablets taken twice daily (McCulloch 2007b).

Drugs that stimulate insulin secretion consist of two major groups known as sulfonylureas and meglitinides. The sulfonylureas are the oldest class of drugs and remain the most widely prescribed for the treatment of hyperglycemia in type 2 diabetics. The mechanism of action of sulfonylureas consists of stimulation of the insulin-producing beta cells found in the pancreas to secrete more insulin. The drug binds to receptors found on the periphery of the beta cells and closes potassium channels. Closing these channels has a stimulatory effect that drives calcium into the cells. The influx of calcium causes insulin release from the beta cells, entering the peripheral circulation to be utilized by organs and skeletal muscle. Although there is an increase in circulating insulin, this class of drugs is not used for type 1 diabetics because their beta cells do not function properly. Studies show that combination therapy with insulin and sulfonylureas does not increase the efficacy of treatment. Type 2 diabetics, however, benefit from the increased release of insulin when long-standing hyperglycemia is not responsive to diet and exercise alone (Masharani, Karam, and German 2004).

There are many drugs that fall under the category of sulfonylureas that differ in dosage, duration of action, and side-effect profiles. Sulfonylureas are oral medications that are taken in tablet form. The first generation sulfonylureas include tolbutamide, tolazamide, acetohexamide, and chlorpropamide. Of these drugs, tolbutamide has the shortest duration of action that ranges from six to twelve hours. Tolbutamide is metabolized into an inactive form by the liver and is safe to use in older patients with poor kidney function. Chlorpropamide has the longest-acting duration of the first-generation sulfonylureas, with effects lasting more than sixty hours. This powerful drug can drop blood sugar levels considerably with the risk of sustained hypoglycemia. Despite the efficacy in reducing glucose levels, there are many side effects common to this drug, causing it to be less frequently prescribed. Acetohexamide has a duration of action that falls between tolbutamide and chlorpropamide and is given in two doses throughout the day. This medication is metabolized by the liver and kidney and must be used with caution in patients with kidney disease (Masharani, Karam, and German 2004).

Second-generation sulfonylureas have a mechanism of action similar to the first generation but are more powerful and require smaller quantities of medication to have an effect. Patients who are prone to the dangerous side effects of hypoglycemia should be carefully considered and examined before administration of second-generation sulfonylureas. This group consists of glyburide, glipizide, and glimepiride, which, like the first-generation drugs, differ in dosage, duration of action, and side-effect profiles. Glyburide comes in tablet form, in doses of 1.25, 2.5, and 5 mg, and is taken in the morning with food. Glyburide is unique in that it not only binds to beta cells of the pancreas but also enters the cells. This increases the duration of action of the drug to more than twenty-four hours. The major side effect of glyburide is a state of hypoglycemia that can be dangerous to the elderly, and therefore it should not be given to patients that are over the age of sixty-five. A better alternative for elderly patients is glipizide, which has a shorter duration of action and is less likely to cause a long-standing hypoglycemic state when compared with glyburide. Glimeperide has a very long duration of action and requires a very low dose to achieve the same glycemic affect as the other second-generation sulfonylureas. It is given as a single dose in the morning during mealtime and has effects lasting upwards of twenty-four hours (Masharani, Karam, and German 2004).

The category of meglitinides has a mechanism of action that is similar to the sulfonylureas by stimulating the secretion of insulin from the pancreatic beta cells. One drug in this category is repaglinide, which has a very short duration of action of three hours. It is orally ingested about fifteen minutes before a meal and provides a burst of insulin with the intent of lowering glucose levels after a meal. Because of its short duration of action and administration before a meal, repaglinide has less of a tendency to cause a state of hypoglycemia that is common in the sulfonylureas. A similar drug, nateglinide, also provides a surge of insulin after a meal, thereby decreasing glucose levels after a meal (Masharani, Karam, and German 2004).

If fasting blood glucose levels cannot be maintained by sulfonylureas alone, the addition of metformin as a combination drug therapy has been proven helpful. Patients with a very high fasting glucose who are taking sulfonylureas have been found to have a benefit from the addition of metformin according to the U.S. Multicenter Metformin Study Group. There was a 2.2 percent decrease in the hemoglobin A1C with the use of combination therapy along with a significant decrease in fasting hyperglycemia. Glucovance is a tablet containing a predetermined combination and is designed for patients who minimize pill consumption. Combination tablets tend to be more expensive and cannot be fine-tuned (McCulloch 2007b).

Thiazolidinediones (TZDs) comprise another category of diabetes drugs that have an effect on sensitivity to insulin by peripheral tissues. The mechanism of action of TZDs affect cells in the periphery by decreasing resistance to insulin along with an increased sensitivity to insulin. Under these effects, peripheral cells begin to express GLUT 1 and GLUT 4 receptors in increased amounts. Hepatocytes in the liver are also affected and decrease glucose output. There are two main drugs within this category, including rosiglitazone and pioglitazone. These drugs have been found to decrease hemoglobin A1C levels by 2 percent when used alone. Rosiglitazone has been found to increase total cholesterol levels along with weight gain. These drugs should be avoided in diabetics with impaired liver function. Patients on these drugs must have blood tests taken every two months for the first year to monitor their liver function (Masharani, Karam, and German 2004).

TZDs, although not a first-line treatment, can be used for treatment of diabetes that is unresponsive to initial therapies including metformin or sulfonylureas. Combinations of TZDs and metformin have proven effective in reducing hemoglobin A1C levels when compared with monotherapy with metformin. Patients who are intolerant to metformin can be placed on a combination of sulfonylureas and a TZD. It has been found that "In a 16-week study of 560 patients with type 2 diabetes who had A1C values greater than 8.0 percent despite sulfonylurea therapy, those receiving pioglitazone (15 or 30 mg) plus the sulfonylurea had significant decreases in A1C values compared with those receiving placebo plus the sulfonylurea" (McCulloch 2007b). Avandaryl and Duetact are examples of tablets that contain combination therapy, reducing the number of pills that a patient has to take daily. Once again, these combination tablets make it difficult to adjust dosages and are more costly to the patient (McCulloch 2007b).

There is another way to control blood glucose levels by controlling the amount of glucose that is absorbed through the intestines. A category of drugs known as alpha glucosidase inhibitors have a mechanism of action that affects intestinal glucose absorption. Acarbose is one drug that falls under this category and is taken daily with meals. When taken properly, acarbose has been found to decrease glucose levels by 50 percent after ingesting food. Although the side-effect profile is minimal, acarbose has been found to cause flatulence in patients and therefore has a high rate of discontinuance. Those patients that do remain on the medication have been found to have a 0.5–1.0 percent decline in hemoglobin A1C levels. Acarbose does not pose a risk for developing hypoglycemia, as do other diabetes medications, and is safe to use in patients that are prone to dangerous hypoglycemia. Miglitol is another drug in this category that has similar effects (Masharani, Karam, and German 2004).

Oral therapy is very commonly used in the treatment of type 2 diabetics. As we have seen, each class of drugs works on a different physiological mechanism and has different potencies as well as side-effect profiles. As a general rule, treatment of type 2 diabetes begins with diet and exercise along with education on risk factors. If hyperglycemia persists, physicians can add various pharmaceutical remedies to the regimen and modify dosage according to the results desired. Complicated cases of diabetes that poorly respond to oral therapy, along with type 1 diabetes, may require the use of insulin injections.

FOCUSING ON INSULIN

To properly protect an individual from fluctuations in blood glucose, it is necessary to frequently check glucose levels and administer medications accordingly (see Figure 4.1). In the 1980s, portable glucose meters were developed, giving new freedoms to the diabetic patient. Diabetics were given the

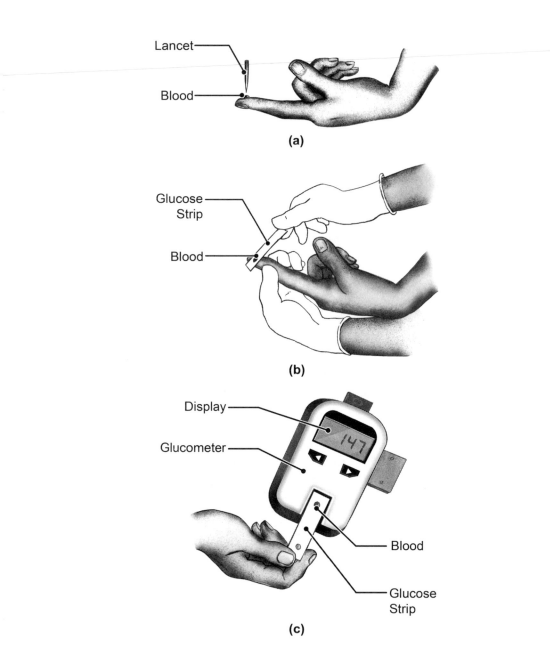

Figure 4.1. Checking blood glucose. A, The finger is pricked with a lancet to produce a drop of blood. B, The blood is transferred to a glucose strip. C, The glucose strip is inserted into a digital glucometer that measures the amount of glucose that is in the bloodstream. Tests are usually performed several times a day to ensure proper glucose levels. *Illustration courtesy of Michael Brookman.*

opportunity to measure blood glucose levels throughout the day in the convenience of their own homes. The increased accuracy of these devices allowed for type 1 diabetics to achieve their primary goal of maintaining glucose levels within a normal range. Checking blood glucose levels several times a day can be burdensome and time consuming; however, individuals who are willing to make this sacrifice will significantly decrease their chances of having diabetic complications. The mechanism of these devices utilizes a single drop of blood frequently taken from the fingertips. The drawn blood is then placed on a testing strip, which contains a chemical that reacts with the blood glucose. Analyzing the results of the chemical reaction, the glucose meter displays a number usually in milligrams per deciliter units onto the screen. Using the information provided by these tests, diabetics can dose and time their insulin injections with precision and accuracy.

As we have already learned, insulin is naturally produced in the body by the beta cells of the pancreas. In type 1 diabetes, this mechanism is disturbed and insulin is not produced in sufficient amounts. Insulin injections are therefore prescribed to type 1 diabetics along with type 2 diabetics to provide a means of controlling blood glucose levels. Type 1 diabetics are reliant on multiple injections of insulin daily because they cannot endogenously produce insulin. In conjunction with blood glucose meters, insulin injections help to maintain blood sugar within normal limits. Insulin is not administered in the oral form because, as a protein, it gets denatured when exposed to the acidic environment of the stomach. Denaturing of insulin alters its configuration, ultimately sacrificing function. To bypass the destructive properties of the stomach, insulin is administered through several injections throughout the day preceding meals.

Insulin therapy is useful in maintaining normal blood glucose levels throughout the day and is customized according to a diabetic's lifestyle and severity of disease. To compensate for the alternating peaks of glucose that occur after meals and dips that occur between meals, different types of insulin have been developed. Insulin comes in various forms that differ in time of onset along with duration of action. Specifically, insulin is divided into four categories, including ultra-short-acting, short-acting, intermediate-acting, and long-acting insulin. Timing of insulin injections is crucial for proper management of diabetes, and injections are usually given fifteen to thirty minutes before food consumption. Improper timing of insulin administration may result in drastic swings in blood sugar, sometimes causing a dangerous condition called hypoglycemia. Hypoglycemia, a state of low blood sugar, can be caused by the administration of too much insulin or insufficient food intake after injection. The increased insulin circulating within the bloodstream causes blood glucose levels to drastically drop, causing the patient to feel dizzy, confused, or even to faint. To counteract the rapidly dropping blood sugar, diabetics are usually advised to carry around emergency foods that can quickly raise levels such as candy or juice.

Insulin injections used to treat individuals with type A1 diabetes come in many forms. Characteristics that determine the type of insulin include time of onset and duration of action. Physicians will prescribe insulin based on the activity and lifestyle of the patient. For example, quick-acting insulin begins to take effect within fifteen minutes of administration but lasts only three to five hours. Long-acting insulin, conversely, takes four to eight hours to take effect but has a duration of action that is twenty to thirty hours longer when compared with quick-acting insulin. A combination of various types of insulin can be used by the diabetic patient to effectively control blood sugar.

Insulin lispro and insulin aspart are two types of ultra-short-acting insulin. This type of insulin is given fifteen to twenty minutes before a meal and has a rapid rate of absorption into the bloodstream. Being absorbed quickly, the action of insulin peaks within an hour and declines within four hours. One adverse side effect of ultra-short-acting insulin is the risk of hypoglycemia if a meal is missed or mistimed. Despite this adverse effect, the fast onset of action has proven to be very convenient to type 1 diabetics, because they can lead more spontaneous lives in regards to their eating schedules. Short-acting insulin includes regular insulin that can be taken thirty minutes before a meal. Regular insulin has a peak effectiveness ranging from one to three hours, with duration of up to seven hours (Masharani, Karam, and German 2004).

Intermediate-acting insulin includes lente and neutral protamine Hagedorn (NPH) insulin. Lente insulin consists of a combination of 30 percent short-acting insulin along with 70 percent long-acting insulin. Intermediate insulin is usually injected twice daily and has an onset of two to four hours, peaking at ten hours (Masharani, Karam, and German 2004).

Insulin can be injected into the abdomen, thighs, upper arms, and buttocks. It is recommended that diabetics rotate injection sites to decrease the risk of injury to one area. However, because each region has a different rate of absorption, rotation should be limited to similar areas on the body. For example, the buttocks have a slower rate of absorption of insulin compared with the upper body and can lead to poor glycemic control and are not generally recommended. The abdomen provides a large area for rotation and provides a consistent rate of insulin utilization (Masharani, Karam, and German 2004).

Insulin injections can be time consuming and painful, decreasing the overall quality of life for diabetics. To increase user friendliness of diabetic care, insulin pumps have been developed, providing an alternative method of administering insulin. Insulin pumps are devices containing insulin worn by the diabetic patient. A piece of tubing connects the device to a needle inserted under the skin, providing a steady flow of insulin into the body, thereby eliminating the need for multiple skin injections. These insulin pumps can be thought of as an external pancreas, providing the body with the proper dosage of insulin throughout the day. Furthermore, they can be programmed to accommodate to an individual's management regimen.

Developments over the past century have given new hope to diabetics, providing them with management options that are both effective and available. The primary objective in the treatment of diabetes is to stabilize and control blood sugar, thereby minimizing risks for both short-term and long-term complications. Achievement of this goal is often very demanding on diabetics. Diabetics must sacrifice a significant amount of time each day monitoring blood glucose levels, administering insulin injections and conforming to diet restrictions. Nonetheless, with careful planning and guidance from a physician, type 1 diabetics are protected against serious pathologic states such as heart disease and even kidney failure. The future of diabetic treatment is involved with devising less invasive methods of testing blood glucose and delivering insulin.

ALTERNATIVES TO CONVENTIONAL DIABETIC CARE*

Diabetes is one of the major illnesses that can be significantly impacted by diet, lifestyle, and supplements. Over the past twenty years, much research has been done on how low glycemic index/load and Mediterranean style diets can help with the stabilization of blood sugar and subsequent hemoglobin A1C regulation. Low glycemic index foods are those that produce only small fluctuations in our blood glucose and insulin levels and are key to preventing weight gain and diabetes. These diets are inherently higher in fish, poultry, lean meats, and nonstarchy vegetables and sparingly include some whole grains that are not milled. The glycemic load allows one to understand how much of that carbohydrate will have an effect on the blood sugar. Although the ADA does not recommend a low-carbohydrate diet, it does state correctly that "use of glycemic index and load may provide a modest additional benefit over that observed when total carbohydrate is considered alone."

The ADA has been rather measured in embracing a higher-protein and lower-carbohydrate diet for diabetics, although the ADA 2007 clinical recommendation states that "dietary carbohydrate is the major determinant of post-

*This section was written by Dr. Zina Kroner, D.O.

prandial glucose levels" (American Diabetes Association 2007). They explain their reasoning by stating that "low-carbohydrate diets might seem to be a logical approach to lowering postprandial glucose. However, foods that contain carbohydrate are important sources of energy, fiber, vitamins, and minerals and are important in dietary palatability" (American Diabetes Association 2007). This statement would be 100 percent correct if the patients had been eating slabs of marbled steak with a side of mayonnaise. Certainly a lean protein with a healthy helping of a variety of vegetables includes the very fiber, vitamins, and minerals that the ADA believes a low-carbohydrate diet would lack.

With regard to the ADA's concern that dietary palatability may be an issue with a low-carbohydrate meal plan, there are dozens of excellent cookbooks that showcase different delectable low-carbohydrate menu choices.

Weight loss is also recommended by the ADA. The ADA website quotes a study that found that, after six months, individuals assigned to low-carbohydrate diets had lost more weight than individuals randomized to low-fat diets (Nordmann et al. 2006). More recent studies depict that a Mediterranean-style diet can help with prevention of cardiovascular risk and optimize blood sugar control.

In addition to dietary modification, supplements can have a significant positive impact on helping to maintain control of blood sugar levels and are increasingly being recognized as key players in the management and prevention of the illness. One such essential dietary mineral is chromium, because its key task is to help the body utilize insulin to burn sugars, carbohydrates, fats, and proteins for energy. Scientists from the Center for Cell Signaling, University of Virginia School of Medicine, have found that chromium works by boosting a certain enzyme called "insulin receptor kinase" (Brautigan, Kruszewski, and Wang 2006), which makes it easier for insulin to bind to cells. Chromium also increases insulin receptor phosphorylation, thereby increasing insulin sensitivity. Optimization of insulin sensitivity is key in diabetic patients being that there is already a significant amount of insulin resistance. It is found in small quantities in foods such as brewer's yeast, calf liver, whole grains, meats, and cheese.

According to 1992 Earth Summit Statistics, U.S. Senate Document no. 264 indicates that the mineral content of the world's farm and range land soil has decreased dramatically. North America, according to this report, has an 85 percent depletion of minerals from its soil during the past one hundred years. This is more than any other continent in the world. The combination of mineral depletion of our soil and America's "dependence" on chromium-free processed foods should encourage physicians to recommend chromium to their patients.

Chromium supplementation in doses ranging between 200 and 1,000 μg daily has been studied in several clinical trials with efficacious results on blood glucose and insulin levels. A study done in 1998 by Dr. Anderson followed 180 men and women with type 2 diabetes. Three different groups of patients on their regular diet received twice daily doses of either 200 or 500 μg of chromium or a placebo. After two months of treatment, those who took 1,000 μg of chromium daily showed significant improvement in insulin response and the number of insulin receptors. The group taking 400 μg of chromium took two months to improve as much as the 1,000 μg group. It should be noted, however, that all the patients taking chromium showed some improvement in diabetic symptomatology (Anderson 1998).

One large human trial compared the effects of 1,000 μg of chromium, 200 μg of chromium, and placebo. Hemoglobin A1C values improved significantly in the group receiving 1,000 μg after two months and in both chromium groups after four months. Fasting glucose was also lower in the group taking the higher dose of chromium (Anderson 1997).

Another study in 2007 published in *Diabetes Care* reviewed the effect of chromium supplementation on glucose metabolism and lipid levels via a literature search conducted on Medline and the Commonwealth Agricultural Bureau. The review showed that, for type 2 diabetics, chromium supplementation improved glycosylated hemoglobin levels by −0.6 percent and fasting glucose by −1.0 mmol/l. No benefit was noted in nondiabetic patients (Balk et al. 2007).

There are several safety considerations with regard to chromium. Although chromium picolinate may improve glycemic control, it may also have an additive effect if combined with medication used by diabetics and may cause blood glucose levels to dip too low. In addition, chromium supplements taken with anti-inflammatory medications such as ibuprofen, indomethacin, naproxen, and aspirin may increase the absorption of chromium in the body. Those patients may have more of a hypoglycemic effect from the chromium. In 1995, a study headed by Diane Stearns, PhD, at Dartmouth College generated controversy about the safety of chromium picolinate. The researchers found that high-dose chromium changed the genetic material of the hamster cells. Critics say that the oxidative stress and DNA damage that was endured occurred because the scientists used doses that were too high. They also argued that administering chromium to cells in test tubes does not have the same biochemical effect as taking chromium supplements orally. No adverse events have been elucidated with short-term chromium use in human studies.

Biotin may improve glucose tolerance and decrease insulin resistance. It has also been found to influence hepatic glucokinase (the enzyme responsible for the first step in glucose utilization in the liver) levels in cell culture. Normally, glucokinase levels are quite low in diabetics. In addition, biotin has been shown to affect pancreatic islet glucokinase activity and insulin secretion in cultured rat islet cells (Furukawa 1999).

Foods that contain some biotin include Brewer's yeast, molasses, egg yolks, milk, liver, soybeans, walnuts, peanuts, wheat bran, and cauliflower. Clinical studies have shown that the combination of chromium picolinate and biotin significantly enhances glucose uptake in skeletal muscle cells and enhances glucose disposal.

One study showed that supplementation with chromium picolinate and biotin can improve glycemic control in patients with type 2 diabetes mellitus with suboptimal glycemic control despite use of oral antihyperglycemic agents. Forty-three patients with impaired glycemic control despite treatments with oral antihyperglycemic agents received either 600 μg of chromium picolinate and 2 mg of biotin while continuing their prestudy oral antihyperglycemic agent. After four weeks, there was a significantly greater reduction in the total area under the curve for glucose during the two-hour oral GTT for the treatment group compared with the placebo group. No adverse effects were reported (Singer and Geohas 2006).

Hypomagnesemia presents more frequently in the diabetic population. Its incidence ranges from 13.6 to 47.7 percent in patients with non-insulin-dependent diabetes. The reasons for this are multifold. According to a recent review article summarizing the causes, the reasons include poor dietary intake, autonomic dysfunction, altered insulin metabolism, glomerular hyperfiltration, osmotic diuresis, recurrent metabolic acidosis, hypophosphatemia, and hypokalemia. Studies show that low magnesium levels have been linked with worsening of glycemic control, coronary artery diseases, hypertension, diabetic retinopathy, nephropathy, neuropathy, and foot ulcerations (Pham et al. 2007).

A study was done to compare the relationship between serum magnesium in diabetic patients with that of forty nondiabetic patients. It was found that serum magnesium levels in diabetic patients were significantly lower than that of controls. Serum magnesium levels were also lower in diabetics with complications vs. those with no complications. Those with long-standing diabetes had lower magnesium levels than those with newer onset diabetes (Frazier 2007).

It is prudent to assess magnesium levels in insulin-resistant and diabetic patients and treat accordingly, taking into account that magnesium requirement are higher in diabetic patients. Magnesium requires daily repletion because of its water-soluble status.

Lipoic acid is found in a variety of foods such as heart and liver meats as well as spinach, broccoli, and potatoes. In the late 1970s, Fredrick C. Bartter, Burton M. Berkson, and associates from the National Institutes of Health (NIH) performed the first human clinical studies using alpha-lipoic acid (ALA) in the United States (Bartter et al. 1980). Intravenous ALA was administered to seventy-nine people with acute and severe liver damage. Full liver function was restored in seventy-five of the patients. Dr. Berkson later used it successfully for the treatment of chronic liver diseases such as viral hepatitis and autoimmune hepatitis (Berkson 1999).

Lipoic acid has been used in diabetic and insulin-resistant patients for many years. ALA's potent antioxidant activity can mitigate some of the long-term effects of the complications of diabetes on the vascular, neurologic, and nephrologic systems. In Germany, lipoic acid has been approved for the treatment of diabetic neuropathy. A recent review article assessed the ability of ALA to improve symptoms of peripheral diabetic neuropathy using a Medline search from 1966 to November 2005. The search showed that ALA appears to improve neuropathic symptoms and deficits when administered via parenteral supplementation over a three-week period. These results should encourage physicians to prescribe this relatively benign and effective treatment option to patients (Foster 2007). ALA has been shown in cell culture experiments to increase cellular uptake of glucose. This occurs as a result of the recruitment of the glucose transporter GLUT 4 to the cell membrane, thereby improving glycemic control (Henriksen 2006).

Animal studies showed that lipoic acid protected pancreatic beta cells from destruction. One trial showed that ALA in doses of 600, 1,200, and 1,800 mg was effective in reducing neuropathic symptoms of diabetic distal symmetric polyneuropathy after five weeks of use (Tang et al. 2007). It is established that, in both an insulin-resistant state and type 2 diabetes, there is an impaired ability of insulin to activate glucose transport in skeletal muscle. Oxidative stress may partially explain this because exposure of skeletal muscle to an oxidant stress leads to impaired insulin signaling. One review article showed that numerous studies demonstrated that "treatment of insulin-resistant animals and type 2 diabetic humans with antioxidants, including alpha-lipoic acid (ALA), is associated with improvements in skeletal muscle glucose transport activity and whole-body glucose tolerance. Endurance exercise training is effective in decreasing skeletal muscle insulin resistance in pre-diabetes and type 2 diabetes. Recent investigations show that the combination of exercise and antioxidant regimens using ALA in animal studies of insulin resistance provide a unique interactive effect that show a greater improvement in insulin action on skeletal muscle glucose transport than either intervention individually. The effect of exercise and ALA is due to improvements in insulin signaling. These studies show that the combination of endurance exercise training and antioxidants help to increase the efficacy insulin resistant skeletal muscle" (Henriksen 2006).

Cinnamon is a small evergreen tree about thirty-five feet tall, native to Sri Lanka and South India. It was imported to Egypt from China as early as 2,000 BC. It was commonly used on funeral pyres in Rome. The Roman Emperor Nero is said to have burned a year's supply of cinnamon at the funeral for his wife in 65 AD.

Cassia, which is a close relative to the cinnamon (true cinnamon) spice but has a less than appealing flavor, has been studied in diabetes. A 2003 study published in the *Diabetes Care* journal followed type 2 diabetics taking 1, 3, or 6 g of cassia daily. All groups had a reduction in mean fasting serum glucose levels from 18 to 29 percent, their triglyceride levels 23 to 30 percent, their low-density lipoprotein cholesterol 7 to 27 percent, and their total cholesterol 12 to 26 percent compared with placebo.

There is suggestion that cassia's significant polyphenol content appears to enhance insulin sensitivity. A study at the USDA Beltsville Human Nutrition Research Center isolated insulin-enhancing complexes in cinnamon. This substance was found to show an decrease in insulin resistance, thereby increasing glucose metabolism twentyfold *in vitro* (Anderson 2004). A recent study shows that the intake of 6 g of cinnamon with rice pudding reduces postprandial blood glucose and delays gastric emptying without affecting satiety (Hlebowicz et al. 2007). Therefore, including 1–2 g of cinnamon with each meal should be considered in the diabetic patient.

5

Diabetes in America and Abroad

THE CULTURAL AND SOCIOECONOMIC
RAMIFICATIONS OF DIABETES

America and the world health community are facing a major health epidemic. Currently, diabetes is the fifth leading cause of death in America. In addition to the almost thirteen million people who are diagnosed, an additional six million Americans suffer but do not know they are diabetics (an estimated 30 percent of those estimated to have the disease do not know they have it). Globally, it is estimated that, at current rates, the prevalence of diabetes will grow by 35 percent from an estimated 135 million in 1995 to 300 million in 2025 (King, Aubert, and Herman 1998). In America, this will result in nearly twenty-two million reported cases of diabetes by 2025. The prevalence of diabetes will continue to be highest in those countries that currently have the highest number of diabetics: China, India, and America. The overall incidence will dramatically increase, however, especially in developing countries where the risk factors for type 2 are becoming more prevalent and education is under funded if at all. Both domestically and abroad, the numbers of people diagnosed with diabetes is growing.

As we have seen in previous chapters, there are both genetic and lifestyle factors that contribute to a person's risk of developing and suffering from the symptoms of diabetes. In Chapter 4, we outlined some of the groups that are most at risk. In this chapter, we will explore how the symptoms and onset of diabetes affects a person's lifestyle and we will ask, "What are the social costs associated with diabetes?"

A DIABETIC'S PERSPECTIVE

I was diagnosed two weeks before my Bat Mitzvah, just before my 13th birthday, on June 1, 1997. Prior to my diagnosis I really didn't know much about diabetes. We have no history of diabetes in my family, so it was a real surprise. The doctors told us later that it may have been caused by an autoimmune reaction triggered by a flu or cold which caused my body to attack the area of the pancreas which creates insulin.

The warning signs were typical, but to us surprising. In my recollection I was not feeling well for a month or so before. I was constantly thirsty, always drinking water, and urinating nonstop. I ate and ate in an attempt to regain energy and stop feeling lethargic, but I lost at least 15 pounds in a month's time.

My family thought I was depressed, had mono, or some other illness. When it came to two weeks before my Bat Mitzvah, my mom saw that there was a dire need to find out what was wrong. When we went to the doctor I described my symptoms and he immediately requested a urine test. The results showed a huge amount of sugar which indicated keto-acidosis. He told us to go get some more tests run at a nearby lab and then to go home, pack and check me into the ER at the local hospital. I was then hooked up to IV's and stayed 3 days in the ICU trying to stabilize my body and blood sugar. I was very dehydrated and had a blood sugar of 547 when I was admitted.

Once I was transferred to a normal room the education began. I learned within the next 3 days how to check my blood sugar, manage food and exercise and more. It was overwhelming yet I knew I had to adapt if I wanted to feel better.

Since then I've seen many changes in the medicines and technology used to manage diabetes. From waiting half and hour before eating a calculated meal after taking regular insulin, the freedom of Humalog which acts much faster on the sugars consumed. I tested the pump for a while but did not like to be attached to my illness. Although I could have maintained good control using the device, it affected me emotionally and I switched back to injections after a year or so. Now with new long acting and short acting insulin, I've learned to adapt and work with my body to maintain control as much as possible.

The treatments have definitely gotten better and have helped me to maintain a great A1C. But it definitely creates a lot of stress and worries, and while it helped me to take better care of myself and respect my body, it definitely limits my ability to enjoy what my friends and family who do not have diabetes enjoy such as food, drink, sleeping late, etc.

I check my blood sugar about 8 times a day, and take a long acting insulin called Levemir twice a day. I maintain a low carbohydrate and low sugar diet, and try to exercise about 4 times a week. While these are healthy habits they definitely create stress in my life. I long to not think about food for just one day. I count carbohydrates and use a scale of one unit to 15 grams when injecting Humalog. I also use the Humalog to correct a high blood sugar.

After 10 years each of these calculations feels almost second nature, yet it definitely takes effort and time. I freely explain what I'm doing to anyone who asks, yet it does get frustrating when those who are afraid of needles get squeamish. What they don't understand is that it's a necessary task to keep me alive and their complaints at seeing a needle but not needing to use one daily are unjustified.

Over the years I've continued to learn more and more about my body and people. Diabetes has both shaped me into the careful, calculated, yet appreciated person I am. It has taught me to respect the simple things in life, act in moderation, and take chances by trusting my gut. It is a complicated disease that definitely influences each person it touches differently. Those who fight it only hurt themselves physically and emotionally, but if you try to work with it you can learn how to control it and learn from the lessons it teaches you. When I was diagnosed we thought that within 10 years there'd be a cure … I'm still waiting. (Danielle B. D.)

The impact on an individual diabetic's life is obviously the most important social effect of diabetes. Medical professionals strive to reduce the discomfort, pain, and inconvenience associated with diabetes and to help the more than eighteen million affected learn to manage their disease and maintain a normal lifestyle. Unfortunately, diabetes is not curable; because so many are forced to live with the disease, proper diagnosis and management are key to managing its symptoms and maintaining a good quality of life. Because diabetes affects both young and old alike and because the two different types of diabetes require such different treatment, the impact on individuals varies considerably. What all diabetics experience, however, is a significant impact on their socioeconomic and social status, as well as many lifestyle restrictions associated with the disease and its symptoms.

Diabetes, if not treated through tight control of blood glucose levels, can lead to severe health complications that are both acute and long term. Acute complications, such as diseases of the blood vessels, are much more likely to be extensive with people suffering from diabetes. In addition, there are specific conditions more likely to affect diabetics such as vision problems and kidney failure. Pregnant women are also at risk for complications from diabetes during their pregnancies. All of these complications vary in their social and socioeconomic impact depending on the patient's age and extenuating risk factors such as lifestyle, education, and race.

No matter the demographic group or type, all of the symptoms of diabetes can lead to lifestyle restrictions that can both contribute to and exacerbate a diabetic's symptoms, not to mention reduce their quality of life. Below we will discuss some of the common restrictions faced by diabetics and how outside factors contribute to quality of life and the overall health of different demographic groups both in America and internationally.

The broadest complication of diabetes to the individual is a loss of quality of life. Quality of life can be defined broadly depending on the person and their cultural background to include activities that give a person pleasure and a sense of positive self-identity. It also includes a person's ability to maintain employment and support themselves and their families. Positive self-image is at risk when a diabetic suffers from weight gain and obesity or is unable to maintain a job. As with many of the complications of diabetes, one factor can contribute to and increase the likelihood of another. Obesity is a primary example because loss of mobility associated with obesity quickly compounds the other vascular problems associated with diabetes.

Obesity is one of four risk factors that contribute to cardiovascular disease. Cardiovascular diseases is the deadliest complication of diabetes and results in the death of more than two-thirds of those suffering from the disease. Studies have shown that people with diabetes are more likely to develop cardiovascular disease than those who do not have it. In fact, people with diabetes have the same risk of coronary heart disease than those who have already had a heart attack. Death rates from heart disease are two to four times higher for diabetics. In addition to obesity, smoking, high cholesterol, and hypertension all combine to form the most dangerous factors for a diabetic in developing cardiovascular disease (King, Aubert, andHerman 1998). Because exercise is one of the key preventative steps in reducing hypertension and obesity, mobility is a key factor in guarding against the most deadly results of diabetes. It is very important that a diabetic be mobile enough to get regular exercise to help prevent obesity and the other complications of a sedentary lifestyle.

Obesity is defined as having as BMI of 30 kg/m2 or greater. Approximately 50 percent of men and 70 percent of women with type 2 diabetes are obese. Obese individuals are three to five times as likely to develop type 2 compared with normal-weight individuals (American Diabetes Association 2007). The longer one is obese, the greater the risk. Despite the high correlation between obesity and diabetes, diabetes is also found amongst individuals who are of normal weight, and some obese people never develop type 2 diabetes. This suggests that other factors such as genetic history play a significant role in one's risk of developing the disease.

The ability to avoid unhealthy weight gain and the many risk factors such as reduced mobility and lack of exercise that accompany it is related to other factors such as a person's overall lifestyle, their socioeconomic status, and their culture. In other words, a diabetics ability to manage their disease it determined by a spectrum of factors that include their education, their ethnic and genetic background, their economic status, their cultural values around diet and exercise, as well as their willingness and ability to exercise regularly.

One stunning example of the dangerous increase in diabetes (and an indicator of the precipitous rise of diabetes) are these sobering statistics: in 1990, the median percentage of the adult population that was obese (BMI > 30) by state was 12 percent; in 2000, this median percentage had grown to 20 percent. According to the World Health Organization, obesity has overtaken AIDS (Acquired immune deficiency syndrome) as the top health problem in the world (King, Aubert, and Herman 1998).

Factors such as diet and exercise as well as lifestyle choices such as drinking and smoking play a very prominent role in the onset and management of the disease and its affect on a person's lifestyle. Lifestyle choices are key in both the risk factors that can lead to diabetes and to the impact it has on a diabetic's life. Diabetes is a disease that can be managed, and, in many cases, the symptoms can be controlled enough to allow a patient to live a life free of any significant restrictions. There will always be some restrictions, however, and these are important indicators of the diabetic's profile and the dynamic that exists between the face of the disease and the identity of the patient.

Some of the most common lifestyle changes that result from diabetes are radical changes in diet and self-medication regimens aimed at controlling the excess of glucose in the system. Later stages of the disease result in more sick days and loss of work productivity and ultimately reduced mobility and death.

Diabetes affects the body's ability to function properly and metabolize food intake. This has two immediate implications. First, it means that a patient must be aware of the role food plays in their life not only biologically (in terms of their metabolic function and caloric intake) both also socially. All cultures and families differ somewhat with how food functions in their daily lives and rituals. Despite these differences, it is a general rule that food plays an integral role in celebrating and maintaining a cultures' tight-knit sense of kinship and community.

It is only within the past quarter century that the NIH has made strong connections between diet and medical problems such as heart disease and diabetes. It is now known definitely that eating healthy foods in moderation is a basic strategy for avoiding obesity and the factors that can accompany it such as diabetes. Despite this increasingly unified medical opinion on unhealthy foods, many families either choose to avoid making healthy dietary choices or are not able to because of economic factors. The ability to make conscious choices about food intake is a major component of how diabetes affects both individuals and larger communities.

In general, a healthy diet aimed at preventing or managing diabetes would include choosing whole grains over processed foods, eating more fruits and vegetables and less fatty meats and dairy, and generally watching portion sizes to avoid weight gain.

One of the most unique aspects of diabetes is the direct everyday role the patient plays in the maintenance of proper glucose levels and therefore their own health. One of the most challenging aspects of providing healthcare is the difficult job of encouraging successful preventative measures in the patient. In much the same way a diabetic suffering from type 2 must take responsibility for their diet and physical fitness, a type 1 diabetic must maintain a daily regimen of testing and monitoring their insulin levels with either injections or a continuous subcutaneous infusion delivered via an insulin pump. In both of these cases, self-medication plays an essential role in the daily health of the patient and their ability to function normally despite their disease.

For most type 1 diabetics, monitoring their glucose level is a daily discipline that takes places before and after meals. In addition to regular times, doctors recommend a diabetic always check their glucose if they experience symptoms such as nausea, persistent thirst, difficulty breathing, or if their blood glucose is more than 300 mg/dl (American Diabetes Association 2007). The importance of regularly checking one's glucose can be inconvenient and does inevitably impact the structure and social fabric of a diabetic's day.

The monitoring and injection of insulin for type 1 diabetics is one of the most prominent and well-known faces of the disease. Certainly seeing a person take a reading using a insulin monitoring device in a public place generates interest and has been portrayed in the popular media and movies. Also, because many more children suffer from type 1 and are forced to use monitoring and injections to treat their diabetes, there may be more sympathy for and awareness of this facet of self-medication. Other more dramatic forms of treatment that are associated with diabetes are kidney dialysis, which is necessitated in later stages of the disease when diabetics can experience kidney disease and ultimately failure. Kidney failure, also known as nephropathy, requires that a dialysis machine be used to remove waste and excess water from the blood (performing the job of the kidneys), dialysis differs depending on the patient's needs, but, in extreme cases of renal failure, the patient must undergo dialysis everyday.

Notwithstanding the importance of these more prominent and popularized forms of self-monitoring and medication, by far the most important and prominent aspect of diabetes is the vital importance of diet and exercise. Indeed, one of the most complex and expensive features of the disease is the importance of daily lifestyle decisions. Because it is so difficult for individuals to maintain the discipline necessary to monitor and moderate their diet, diabetes is one of the most difficult diseases to treat long term. This necessitates a two-fold dynamic. The first vital component is education; the second is maintaining strict guidelines for follow-up and preventative measures.

A COSTLY MATTER

The cost of diabetes can be measured in both direct and indirect medical expenditures. Some of the most important direct costs are medical treatment and hospital stays, whereas indirect costs include lost productivity at work, permanent disability, and premature mortality.

One excellent indicator of both the direct economic and social cost of diabetes is the volume of doctor's visits. In 2002 (the most recent year data are available), there were 62.6 million office visits to physicians, 44 million home visits, 5.9 million hospital outpatient visits, 5 million hospice care days, and 5 million emergency rooms visits. Of these, an estimated four million were related to cardiovascular disease; that makes up 24 percent of the total hospital days attributable to diabetes. Of these, the great majority of hospital visits are by those diabetics who are sixty-five years of age or older (American Diabetes Association 2007).

In addition to the volume of visits, there are additional criteria that can be used to evaluate costs incurred. For example, according to the American Diabetic Association, people who have risk factors for diabetes should be tested once every three years. For those who have failed a glucose fasting test, they should be tested yearly because up to 8 percent of them will develop diabetes. Almost fifty-four million Americans are pre-diabetic and should monitor their health and the symptoms associated with diabetes on a regular basis and with a thorough knowledge of what to look for. Promoting this awareness requires education, which is a significant indirect cost associated with diabetes (American Diabetes Association 2007).

Another direct cost is the testing that must occur to determine whether someone is diabetic or pre-diabetic. A new genetic test developed by DeCode

Genetics in April 2007 was developed that can identify people with an increased risk of developing type 2. The test, which costs more than $500, is both expensive and cannot predict diabetes definitively. One important attribute of the tests is that the results can encourage those at higher risks to commit themselves to lifestyle changes and preventative measures (Grady 2006).

Education is one of the most significant and under-funded costs associated with diabetes. Education is one of the primary issues that governs the profile and impact of diabetes both in America and globally. For an average individual, knowledge of key risk factors associated with diabetes are fundamental in prevention and management. Most of these factors have already been mentioned: diet, exercise, symptoms of pre-diabetes, and genetic predisposition are essential components of a comprehensive education of the public. If a population or community does not understand the importance of these factors, the risk of diabetes to that community increased exponentially.

In addition to what information must be disseminated, the other key question is how? How local and national governments can best facilitate education and outreach is one of the most pressing concerns of public health professionals and physicians. As the numbers of diabetics grows, and increasingly children are at risk, the pressure to develop effective outreach and education has become paramount.

Many argue that, in addition to education, the government should intervene and legislate some basic rules regarding the health of various foods. Local municipalities have tried to pursue this strategy by removing soda machines from schools and replacing them with vending machines that serve juices. In addition, more aggressive legislation is being considered in various states and counties. One such example of this is New York City trying to ban the use of trans fatty acids in restaurants and delis. Although many have fought against such regulation, claiming that it is overreaching by the government or that it will reduce the quality of food, the pressure to serve healthy food seems to be on the winning side. As of the spring of 2007, major fast food chains such as KFC have switched from using "trans fats" to healthier vegetable oils (Aubrey 2006).

Although government regulation will no doubt help, more localized community outreach and education is vitally important. One such program that has shown signs of success is a process by which a new sector of healthcare practitioner known as "Diabetic Educators" are trained and certified to monitor and educate a localized population of diabetics. Needless to say, implementing this new level of monitoring in expensive, but studies have shown that consistent monitoring and support of diabetics is a cost-effective way of improving maintenance and preventative care.

Studies have consistently shown that educating people about the risks of diabetes and its causes can significantly improve awareness. Awareness of how specific factors such as diet and other lifestyle choices increase one's risk of developing type 2 diabetes is the first step in reducing those risks and developing a healthier lifestyle. Other possible avenues of education are literature and the internet, both of which have been developed by organizations such as the not-for-profit ADA as well as the World Health Organization.

Education must answer the following questions when addressing people at high risk for developing diabetes. (1) How does losing weight help a diabetic? (2) What is fat and how does diet affect diabetes? (3) Why is body image and exercise important?

Weight loss helps people with diabetes in two important ways. First, it lowers insulin resistance. This allows their natural insulin (in people with type 2 diabetes) to do a better job lowering blood glucose levels. Losing weight lowers blood glucose and may allow a diabetic to reduce the amount of glucose they are taking, or quit taking it altogether. Second, it improves blood fat and blood pressure levels. People with diabetes are about twice as likely to get cardiovascular disease as most people. Lowering blood fats and blood pressure is a way to reduce that risk (American Diabetes Association 2007).

When most people think of an obese person, they think of fat. Indeed, obese people are regularly referred to disparagingly as fat in popular culture and on the street, but fat is more than just a description of being overweight. Fat is a complex factor in the average American's diet and contributes dramatically to their health problems.

In the body, excess fat is typically an indication of more caloric intake than expenditure. In the diet, fat is one of many essential nutrients. Dietary fat is the most "fattening" nutrient we eat. It provides 9 cal, units of energy, per gram. Carbohydrates and proteins each provide 4 cal/g (Clark 2003). Dietary fat is divided into two types: saturated (which is solid at room temperature) and unsaturated (liquid at room temperature).

It is the saturated fats that are most dangerous and need to be monitored in one's diet. Saturated fats and trans fats act very much the same, increasing your risk of heart disease and contributing to obesity. Unfortunately, it is these fats that are also commonly found in processed foods and fast foods. When an individual or family is on a restricted budget and eats processed or fast foods and/or enjoys certain ethnic foods such as deep fried meats and breaded items, their risk of a high-fat diet escalates. Fat in this case is linked to both one's diet and culture, as well as one's economic status and accessibility to quality fresh foods (Tripp-Reimer et al. 2001).

One factor in the rise of diabetes is the popularity of fast food and preprocessed foods. Preprocessed foods are popular because both they are easy to prepare (or order) and, as a rule, they are cheaper than fresh fruits and vegetables. The ADA as well as the USDA (which establishes nutritional guidelines in the United States) advocate that American diets emphasize fruit and fresh vegetables. Unfortunately, access to fresh food can often be restricted as a result of economic pressures and other factors that limit availability in both urban neighborhoods and rural towns. As an alternative, many families have in the past relied on canned vegetables and fruits, but these have been implicated in a number of high-risk factors because canned and preprocessed food available at many markets tend to be higher in sugar and sodium, additives that dramatically increase the likelihood of a person developing early symptoms of type 2 diabetes as well as other risk factors such as obesity, high cholesterol, and high blood pressure (Tripp-Reimer et al. 2001).

Related to food intake but perhaps more complicated by society and one's culture is the way individuals and social groups view body types. "Body type" is a general term used to describe both a person's height and weight but also more subjective factors such as their proportions and the way they dress, their different styles, etc.

Although differing perceptions of body type is a natural manifestation of different cultural traditions, it also complicates the awareness and diagnosis of diabetes because different people view physical indicators such as obesity differently.

What is important about body image is that it can sometimes make people more aware if they have a weight problem. Of course, the opposite can be true and people can be overly focused on and negative about their body image, a fixation that also can be bad. However, body image is important because it significantly determines an individual's awareness of their body and therefore of vital factors that affect the development of diabetes. For those who do not pay any attention to their bodies, the risks are higher.

Below are three symptoms associated with type 2 diabetes and obesity that can lead to debilitating health symptoms and lifestyle restrictions such as loss of mobility, work, and sexual function, and complications of pregnancy.

Mobility is not only a factor in heart disease and stroke. It is also a key factor in diabetic neuropathy or nerve damage. Nerve damage affects 60–70 percent of people with type 1 and type 2 diabetes. It is most common amongst men and those who have been affected by diabetes for a long time. Diabetic neuropathy can affect almost every region of the body but most commonly results in peripheral neuropathy that leads to the loss of feeling in the legs, feet, and hands (American Diabetes Association 2007). The result of this loss of feeling can be both immediate and dire. Not only does it restrict movement and lead to a diabetic being immobilized or bound to a wheelchair, but it can result in injuries, especially to the feet, that can go unnoticed, leading to complications and possible amputation.

Diabetic nephropathy is the leading cause of patients undergoing dialysis for end-stage renal disease and is the underlying cause of nontraumatic lower-extremity amputations in diabetic patients.

Autonomic neuropathy affects nerves that are not consciously controlled, for example, regulating heartbeat, blood pressure, and digestion. The possible results of automatic neuropathy can be severe as well as dramatically reduce a diabetic's quality of life. Perhaps chief amongst these symptoms is impotence, which affects 13 percent of men with type 1 diabetes and 8 percent of men with type 2. In addition to sexual dysfunction, autonomic neuropathy can also impair a diabetic's ability to adequately process and move food through the digestive system, urinary tract infections, and damage to the nerves in the heart, which can lead to myocardial infarction (heart attack without symptoms) and resultant sudden death (American Diabetes Association 2007).

Peripheral vascular disease is a serious complication of both type 1 and type 2 diabetes that results in reduced blood flow and oxygen to tissues in the legs and feet.

Nearly 60 percent of the nontraumatic lower-extremity amputations in the United States occur in people with diabetes. The risk of amputation is fifteen to forty times greater in individuals with diabetes than without. From 2000 to 2001, almost 82,000 nontraumatic lower-extremity amputations were performed on people with diabetes (American Diabetes Association 2007).

Although it is impossible to divorce one's physical health from one's socio-economic well being, it is important when considering diabetes impact to pay careful attention to the different vectors of a person's life and how social factors contribute to both the risk of diagnosis and proper diabetes management.

In addition to the severe restrictions caused by diabetic neuropathy, autonomic neuropathy, and peripheral vascular disease, other symptoms such as depression can profoundly affect a diabetic's health and well-being. Indeed, there is a direct correlation between loss of mobility, sexual function, and the ability to hold a job and depression.

For any education program to be successful, it must be tailored to meet both the physical and psychological challenges faced by diabetics and those at risk of developing diabetes.

DISCRIMINATION

In addition to preventative measures and outreach, public policy and education programs must also recognize how social factors such as poverty, racial and economic discrimination, and ignorance contribute to and complicate the effects of diabetes and profoundly affect those who suffer from the disease. These costs are complicated to categorize because they affect every sector of the economy and every strata of society.

Discrimination has proven to be one of the most difficult problems to address and solve. Perhaps its most profound impact is how discrimination contributes to poverty and its many companion implications, including poor diet and life-style habits, substandard education, and preventative healthcare and depression. The costs of these factors will be discussed at length below. The implications of racial discrimination will be discussed below, in "Diabetes in America."

Diabetics experience discrimination in a variety of ways and places. One way diabetics have historically been discriminated against regardless of race or gender is by being barred from certain employment or from receiving proper medical care. To help fight this kind of discrimination, different lawsuits have been filed in court. Many of these lawsuits have resulted in expanding the protection of diabetics in the workplace. Some examples of these lawsuits that have resulted in the protecting of a diabetic's rights include mandating that any teacher or educator whose responsibilities might put them in contact with a diabetic be educated about the needs of a diabetic student. Similar cases have been filed on behalf of incarcerated diabetics whose care must be entrusted to the correctional institution where they are held (Shereen Arent 2003). This means that they would have access to a proper diet and monitoring equipment and other vital controls that are necessary to manage their disease. Other issues that have been raised about the rights of diabetics are whether diabetics are fit to serve as police officers or commercial truck drivers. In both cases, court decisions have awarded diabetics the right to apply for and work in these areas.

Because of these and other court victories and outreach to promote awareness about discrimination against diabetics, the ADA reports that the number of inquiries they receive has grown dramatically. This rise, they argue, points to the success of their educational efforts and the rise of awareness about the discrimination faced by diabetics (American Diabetes Association 2007).

Diabetics have faced discrimination in the workplace and other public sectors where they sometimes need special dispensation to manage their disease. Various organizations have been very aggressive and successful in raising the public awareness of diabetes and arguing that diabetics, with proper treatment, are capable of fulfilling the most complex and sensitive jobs professionally and without danger to themselves or others. There is another way diabetics face discrimination, however, and it has far greater social costs and is much more difficult to address. It is the problem of racial and economic discrimination.

OUTCOME OF INCOME

Poverty affects many different aspects of diabetes and diabetics in America and around the world. Diabetes can both exacerbate the factors that contribute to the onset of type 2 as well as contribute to disability that in turn can result in greater financial hardship and the greater risk of eventual poverty.

One of the most troubling features of diabetes is how it tends to strike at lower income families. What makes this especially tragic is the way diabetes can contribute to poverty, thereby afflicting those struggling for financial stability with a double burden of disease and poverty, an insidious cycle. This is a complex phenomenon related both to long-standing inequalities in America's economy that affect minority populations and cultural traditions that govern diet and exercise.

In America, as of January 2002, there were an estimated 122,000 people aged eighteen to sixty-four years receiving benefits as part of Social Security Disability in which diabetes is listed as the primary basis of disability. Another 109,000 people aged eighteen to sixty-four years received Social Security Disability Index benefits in which diabetes is listed as the secondary basis of their disability. The number of unemployed people with diabetes who are not receiving Social Security Disability Index but who would be employed in the absence of diabetes is unknown. An estimated 176,475 person-years of permanent disability in 2002 are attributable to diabetes. Each case of permanent disability results in an average lost earnings of $42,462 per year. The national cost estimate excludes the cost to family and friends caring for a person with permanent disabilities attributable to diabetes. This number is estimated to be considerably higher and can be seen as a primary factor in the risk of poverty faced by extended families with one or more diabetic (American Diabetes Association 2007).

In general, poverty has been under recognized as contributing to the prevalence of diabetes, but this is changing. In part, the greater awareness of how poverty increases a person's risk of developing diabetes has been in response to the dramatic rise in diabetes in minority and indigenous populations, groups that historically are also lower income and victims of poverty.

The International Diabetes Federation (IDF) has stated unequivocally that indigenous populations around the world are often marginalized and treated with indifference or even hostility by mainstream societies, noting that these groups are also socially disadvantaged and many live in poverty and are therefore at greatly increased risk of a number of chronic diseases (including type 2 diabetes and associated vascular disease and renal failure). The IDF has further stated that poverty and obesity are inextricably intertwined, pointing to how, in western societies, poor quality diets (high in fat and refined carbohydrates) cost less than high quality diets (rich in lean meats and fish and fresh fruit and vegetables), a hidden feature of poverty that contributes directly to diabetes and other public health crises (American Diabetes Association 2007).

The correlation between poverty and diet is more complex than just the relationship between the high cost of good food vs. the relative affordability of foods high in refined sugars and fats. For many of America's poorest families, the U.S. government subsidy and welfare programs provide actual food staples. These foodstuffs are in turn manufactured with agricultural products that have been subsidized by the government. Corn is traditionally one of the most heavily subsidized of these foods, and corn products, including corn syrup, are found in disproportionately high levels in cheap heavily processed foods.

The importance of aggressive education and preventative health programs has been firmly established. How to best implement these programs is still a difficult and controversial subject. A number of barriers exist that prevent the adoption and implementation of new and more effective methods of patient care. These include (1) healthcare provider knowledge; (2) communication between patient and healthcare provider; (3) attitudes and beliefs of the patient, community/culture, healthcare provider, and healthcare system; (4) racial and ethnic disparities; (5) variations in settings, including the healthcare system; (6) clinical traditions; (7) socioeconomic status; and (8) cost (Davidson 2003).

Despite the studies that show increased nursing and outsourced care would dramatically improve the management of diabetes and prevention of pre-diabetic patients, there is a significant financial barrier. The most difficult and obvious question is who will pay for nurse-directed care? Although better diabetes care translates into decreased long-term medical costs, this savings may take a long time to materialize. Unfortunately, only a few committed organizations are willing to assume the initial cost with an eye toward future savings. This is a serious problem because the cost of diabetes is increasing rapidly and the cost of its complications is predicted to overwhelm the current American medical system.

The most direct and effective method of confronting these growing complications and patients is by meeting the evidence-based ADA guidelines. The question remains how best to educate communities (American Diabetes Association 2007).

DIRECT AND INDIRECT COSTS

In general, the many restrictions that can result from both type 1 and type 2 diabetes can lead to significant results for both their physical and mental health as well as their socioeconomic status. The costs associated with both of these restrictions are discussed below.

In addition to the limitations diabetes can have on a person's mobility and health, there are a host of other implications that can profoundly affect an individuals lifestyle. The first of these is the tremendous cost of diabetes.

In American, direct medical expenditures are growing, totaling $92 billion up from $44 billion in 1997. The total estimated cost of diabetes in 2002 in both direct and indirect costs was $132 billion. This is approximately 18 percent of the total U.S. personal healthcare expenditures. The rate of diabetes is growing as can be seen in the same figures from 1998, which report that the direct and indirect costs were $98 million an estimated 8 percent of the overall expenditures made for personal healthcare expenditures (American Diabetes Association 2007).

Indirect costs or those costs from lost workdays, restricted mobility, or permanent disability and death caused by diabetes are a huge drag on individuals' economic stability. In 2002, these costs totaled $48 billion. On average, controlling for age, men with diabetes have 3.1 more lost work days and 7.9 more bed days than those who do not.

Direct costs refer to the immediate medical expenditures associated with treating diabetes and diabetes-related illnesses. In 2002, direct costs totaled $91.8 billion and comprised $23.2 billion for diabetes care, $24.6 billion for chronic complications attributable to diabetes, and $44.1 billion for excess prevalence of general medical conditions. Inpatient days (43.9 percent), nursing home care (15.1 percent), and office visits (10.9 percent) constituted the major expenditures according to specific services. In addition, 51.8 percent of direct medical expenditures were incurred by people sixty-five years or older (American Diabetes Association 2007).

Diabetes-related hospitalization was estimated at $92 billion for 2002. This is a significant increase from the $44 billion in 1997 (American Diabetes Association 2007).

People with diabetes have medical expenditures that are on average 2.5 times higher than they would if they did not have diabetes. Per capita medical expenditures totaled $13,243 for people with diabetes and $2,560 for people without diabetes. In total, $40.3 billion was spent for impatient hospital care and $13.8 billion for nursing home care for people with diabetes.

Diabetes-related hospitalization totaled 16.9 million days in 2002. Rates of outpatient care are highest for physician office visits, which included 62.6 million visits to treat people with diabetes. Cardiovascular disease is the most costly complication of diabetes, accounting for more than $17.6 billion of the $91.8 billion direct medical costs for diabetes in 2002 (American Diabetes Association 2007).

One added complication for Americans suffering from diabetes is insurance. There are an estimated forty-one million Americans who do not have insurance. For those without health insurance, diabetes can be a frightening prospect. Although no hard data exist, the ADA has increased its outreach to those diabetics without insurance and anecdotally has noted a dramatic increase in the calls coming into their call center (American Diabetes Association 2006).

Despite the heavy psychological toll and estimated $132 billion total costs associated with diabetes in the United States, it is widely held that the true cost is much higher. The true economic burden of diabetes must take into account factors difficult to asses such as pain and suffering, care provided by nonpaid caregivers, and several areas of healthcare spending in which people with diabetes probably use services at higher rates than people without diabetes (e.g., dental care, optometry care, and the use of licensed dietitians). In addition, the overall cost estimate excludes undiagnosed cases of diabetes, an estimated 30 percent of the overall diabetic population. Regardless, healthcare spending in 2002 for people with diabetes is more than double what spending would be without diabetes (American Diabetes Association 2007). Diabetes imposes a substantial cost burden to those individuals with diabetes and their families. Eliminating or reducing the health problems caused by diabetes could significantly improve the quality of life for people with diabetes and their families while at the same time potentially reducing national expenditures for healthcare services and increasing productivity in the U.S. economy. To deal directly with the many factors that contribute to diabetes, a consortium of local and national organizations must promote better preventive care and education, more widespread diagnosis, and more intensive disease management.

In addition, larger social problems such as poverty must be addressed to more fully confront the causes of diabetes. How these contributing factors define diabetes in America and how the demographics of diabetes portend many of its future issues will be addressed in Chapter 6.

DIABETES IN AMERICA

According to the ADA, there are over twenty million people who have diabetes in the United States. Of these, almost one-third or 6.2 million people do not know they have diabetes. In addition, more than fifty-four million are considered at risk for diabetes or are pre-diabetic.

If current trends continue, one in three Americans and one in two minorities born in 2000 will develop diabetes in their lifetime. Every day, approximately 4,110 people are diagnosed as diabetic. Since 1987, the death rate attributable to diabetes has increased by 45 percent, whereas the death rates attributable to heart disease, stroke, and cancer have declined (American Diabetes Association 2007).

Given the huge percentage of Americans who will contract diabetes or have to adopt restrictive lifestyle choices to control pre-diabetic factors, awareness of diabetes is rising in America. This awareness is not only attributable to the rising number of diabetics but also to a general social awareness of the importance of healthy lifestyle choices such as diet and exercise. Despite this awareness, however, the numbers are expected to continue to rise amongst all American ethnic groups but especially among minority populations.

Of all the factors that contribute to an American's risk of developing diabetes today, race plays the dominant role; statistics show that ethnic minorities are disproportionately affected. There are four race/ethnicity categories used by medical professionals to chart rates of diabetes. These are Hispanic, non-Hispanic white, non-Hispanic black, and non-Hispanic other. In 2000, non-Hispanic black women had the highest prevalence among people less than seventy-five years old. Between 1997 and 2000, the prevalence of diabetes increased more than 10 percent among non-Hispanic white males and non-Hispanic black females, whereas increases were smaller in other race/ethnic and gender groups (American Diabetes Association 2007).

Although the risks have grown amongst Hispanics and non-Hispanic blacks, the highest rates have affected Native Americans. Type 2 diabetes is considered a full-blown epidemic in Native American populations, and the overall rates of diagnosis in native populations are equal to or higher than the rates in any other group. Despite the overall rates, the prevalence in particular tribes varies dramatically. The highest rates of diabetes in the United States, as well as the world, are located amongst the Pima Indians of Arizona. Amongst the Pima tribe, almost 65 percent of men and women aged forty-five to seventy-four are diagnosed with type 2 diabetes (American Diabetes Association 2007).

In January 2006, *The New York Times* ran a series of articles titled "Bad Blood" that spotlighted the social consequences of diabetes. One of the main points of the series was that type 2 diabetes is an epidemic that promises to grow widely, but its consequences are seriously underappreciated because the disease's victims are disproportionately poor people of color. Citing the report made by the Centers for Disease Control and Prevention (CDC) that project that one in three children born in 2000 will become diabetic at sometime in their lives, the *Times* showed that, in New York City, income has a significant impact on a child's risk of diabetes. It showed that, among children who live below 96th Street on the Upper East Side, with a median income of $75,000 and a poverty rate of 6.2 percent, only 1 percent of the population has diabetes. This was contrasted with the neighborhood of Spanish Harlem (located no more than a mile away), where the median income is $20,000 and the poverty rate of 38.2 percent and a whopping 16 percent of children have diabetes (Kleinfield 2006).

As we have seen, diet and the traditions around food are deeply rooted in history and culture. Social scientists have long recognized that food choices and modes of eating reflect symbolic, affective, familial, and gender-specific associations. Although different ethnic groups possess unique traditions, the American diet is a combination of many cultures and cuisines. To understand American dietary habits fully, one must not only study the traditional foods and food habits of the many minority groups but also the interaction between the majority culture and the cultures of these smaller groups.

For many minority cultures living in the United States, maintaining a strong connection to their culture of origin is paramount and puts added importance on rituals and events that often center around eating food.

One study that investigated the links between ones' culture and perceptions of food focused on African American women with type 2 diabetes. This study showed that, for many African American women, modifying dietary patterns is particularly challenging given the highly ritualized nature of eating and food selection and the meanings encoded in foods and food-centered events in their communities.

One of the most significant findings in the study was the importance of properly educating healthcare providers about the cultural aspects of food consumption so they can understand how a culture's history helps determine food patterns. The study concluded with the observation that this education is key for healthcare workers to successfully work in partnership with people with type 2 diabetes to shift their cultural norms toward healthy eating (Liburd 2003).

Another important recent study focused on the eating habits of South and West Asian Indian immigrants in the United States over a five-year period. It has shown that the diets of a majority in this community changed from one featuring low-fat, high-fiber foods to one characterized by higher-fat animal protein, low fiber, and high levels of saturated fat. This study further revealed that, consistent with the diets of all other ethnic groups in the United States, there is an increased tendency among Asian Indians in America to consume fast foods and convenience foods as a way of saving time. Also, these changes in habit reflect their changing economic and cultural priorities (Kulkarni 2004).

One significant but largely hidden cost of diabetes is depression. Studies have shown that up to 25 percent of members of ethnic minority groups with diabetes also are susceptible to depression and for major depressive disorders. Furthermore, minorities display higher levels of the symptoms of depression than those found in members of majority groups. The repercussions of these depressive symptoms have been shown to affect disease management, and new data suggest that they may directly reduce insulin sensitivity. The study concludes that depression most likely influences glycemic control through both behavioral and physiological pathways, highlighting at least two targets for intervention (Trief et al. 2006).

Related to the relationship between depression and diabetes, one recent study has explored how environmental factors contribute to both the advent and progression of the disease. Healthcare professionals are increasing their focus on the environmental factors associated with the control of diabetes, but, so far, few researchers have examined the impact of endemic stress on diabetes self-care and psychological functioning. Endemic stress is defined as a heightened awareness of stressful life events for marginalized individuals. Endemic stress, for example, acknowledges that the daily life experiences, including stressors, of African Americans are greatly affected by racism, oppression, and discrimination emerging from several external sources, such as economic, political, social, and physical environmental condition (Trief et al. 2006).

Although these factors are likely to operate for all women regardless of race or ethnicity, studies have found that certain experiences, such as racism, are unique to women of color, particularly African American women. Health professionals need to consider social, environmental, and individual factors to understand and treat women's chronic and psychological health, and such information is also useful in prescribing treatment and designing programs and approaches that will foster profound effects and lasting benefits.

African Americans aged twenty years or older are twice as likely to have type 2 diabetes as whites of similar age, and statistics show that they are at greater risk of morbidity and mortality from the diseases. The differential effects of diabetes on African Americans may be attributed to the fact that this population must balance the demands associated with managing a major chronic illness in the midst of multiple stressors occurring in several different domains of their lives. The manifestation of these stresses may manifest in overall reduction of their psychological and physical health.

In addition to race, genetic predisposition/family history is also a key factor in both type 1 and 2 diabetes. Studies have shown that genetic factors play a major role in the likely onset of type 2 diabetes. In addition, brothers and sisters of children of those with type 1 have a 10 percent chance of developing diabetes by age sixty, and, for North American whites with first-degree relatives (parents, siblings, and offspring), the risk of developing type 1 before age thirty is 1–6 percent. In contrast, the likelihood of developing diabetes without a family member with type 1 is less than 0.3 percent (American Diabetes Association 2007).

When evaluating rates of diabetes among different populations, it is important to understand the difference between the terms "prevalence" and "incidence." The prevalence of diabetes is a term that refers to the total number of people known to have diabetes at a particular time. For example, the prevalence of diabetes in 1980 was six million, whereas in 2002, it was almost thirteen million. The incidence of diabetes, however, refers to the new cases diagnosed in a particular time period. The prevalence of a disease reflects it burden on society and its social costs, whereas incidence refers to its growth and development.

We have already noted that the prevalence of diabetes in America is roughly eighteen million. Amongst women under forty-five, the prevalence of diagnosed diabetes increased almost 33 percent between 1997 and 2000. Amongst other age groups, the prevalence of diabetes remained the same. Amongst men, however, the overall prevalence rose in every age category and showed the greatest relative increase among men aged sixty-five to seventy-four (American Diabetes Association 2007).

In 1994, fourteen states had a prevalence of diagnosed diabetes of less then 4 percent, and only two states had a prevalence of 6 percent or higher. By 2002, the rates of diabetes had risen dramatically, no state had less than 4 percent, and twenty-nine states, Puerto Rico, and the District of Columbia had rates of 6 percent or higher. Across America, the prevalence of diabetes tends to be greater in the south and eastern regions than in the west. The prevalence of diabetes increased 10 percent between 1994 and 2002, and amongst all the states that kept data, the prevalence rose at least 50 percent within that time period (American Diabetes Association 2007).

Although race and gender are significant, age is still the biggest factors in determining the risk of diabetes. Amongst Americans aged twenty years or older, 20.6 million or 9.6 percent of all people in this age group have diabetes. Amongst those aged sixty years or older, 10.3 million or 20.9 percent have diabetes. For those suffering from diabetes, the risks associated with almost all aspects of the disease become more pronounced and have greater ramifications the older the diabetic.

Perhaps no statistic more dramatically highlights the role diet and obesity plays in the risks of diabetes than the following: people at increased risk of adult-onset type 2 diabetes can prevent or delay the onset of the disease by losing 5–6 percent of their body weight through diet and exercise. The correlation is clear: excess weight increases your risk of diabetes.

Despite the clear correlation between maintaining a proper diet and BMI, obesity continues to contribute to diabetes. Why? One basic reason is economic: energy-dense foods are the cheapest option for the consumer according to a study conducted on the link between calories and obesity. The correlation between money and diet means that, as long as healthier food are more expensive, obesity, as a result of calorie-dense processed food, will continue to be a problem for the working poor.

Government efforts to address diet-related health problems among low-income Americans have done little to reduce incidence of obesity and diabetes. One reason may be that, even when they do account for the economics of different types of foods, such programs often neglect other pressures faced by low-income families (American Diabetes Association 2007).

In 1999, for example, the USDA began promoting a revised "Thrifty Food Plan," designed to help people choose low-cost, healthy foods. However, as Diego Rose of Tulane University's Department of Community Health Sciences showed in a 2004 study, the plan failed to account for time stresses on working-class families. Rose calculated that it would take an average of sixteen hours per week to prepare the meals outlined in the Thrifty plan and that working women tended to have only about six hours per week to devote to the kitchen at the time the plan was unveiled (Mendoza 2007).

INTERNATIONAL INTERPRETATION

Just as in America, the costs and prevalence associated with diabetes are predicted to rise precipitously across the globe over the next three decades; this rise is expected in both developed and developing nations. Both the direct costs of treatment and the indirect costs of lower productivity and decreasing public health are scheduled to increase.

The number of adults with diabetes in the world is estimated to increase by 122 percent, from 135 million in 1995 to 300 million in 2025. There will be a 42 percent increase, from 51 million to 72 million, in the developed countries. Meanwhile, in the developing countries, there will be a 170 percent increase, from 84 million to 228 million. By the year 2025, more than 75 percent of all people with diabetes will be in the developing countries compared with 62 percent in 1995 (Wild et al. 2004).

The highest increases in prevalence between 1995 and 2025 will be for China (68 percent) and India (59 percent).The highest rates of prevalence will not change between today and 2025. In 2025, the three countries with the largest number of people with diabetes will remain India, China, and the United States. Although the developed nations will continue to lead the world in the prevalence of diabetes, overall the incidence of diabetes will grow more in developing countries (Wild et al. 2004).

Worldwide, diabetes has now become an epidemic, affecting more than 230 million people or 6 percent of the world's adult population. This number is expected to exceed 350 million in less than twenty years if action is not taken (Wild et al. 2004).

The reasons for this increase are complex but mirror many of the same social and economic phenomenon that we have seen in the United States, most notably diet and lifestyle.

These same factors have historically separated different countries and cultural groups. That being said, the rise of the global economy and international cross-culturalism has created a perfect climate for exchanging ideals about diet and exercise. The importance of lifestyle to the rise of diabetes begs the question of whether some countries and nationalities have had historically lower rates of diabetes (Wild et al. 2004).

The answer is that, yes, historically many different cultures and ethnic groups had lower rates of diabetes. The reasons for this lower prevalence are diverse. The most basic answer is that traditionally, before the advent of the global economy and preprocessed foods, most people ate more simply, exercised more, and had fewer cases of obesity. In this respect, rates of diabetes can be seen growing across the globe as access to higher fat and processed foods becomes more commonplace. In addition to availability, cultural attitudes toward different ethnic foods has become more liberal so that it is not unusual for American-style fast food outlets to compete with more traditional food sources all around the world.

The greater availability of processed foods comes at a time when many cultures are participating in more sedentary lifestyles such as working in offices or factories, a combination that again limits exercise and increases the likelihood of obesity and pre-diabetic factors.

In some ways, the global economy has brought with it greater prosperity. In other ways, however, it has increased many pressures on traditional cultural bonds. For example, as more and more of the economy is governed by international companies, many citizens are no longer in a position to grow their own food. Because the costs of perishable fresh food is high around the world, this move away from gardening or agriculture is in effect a move away from regular fresh food. This too has contributed to a decline in the health of many populations and can be seen as a kind of poverty. In addition to diet, lack of basic aid reduces the chance of diabetic and pre-diabetic populations of getting adequate treatment (Wild et al. 2004).

As in America, poverty has been under recognized as a contributor to prevalence of type 2 diabetes. One source of compelling data is from Britain where a recent study cross-checked mortality rates from diabetes (known to be seriously under recorded) with rates of insulin therapy in the inner cities. The study showed that patients in more deprived areas were more likely to suffer from diabetic and pre-diabetic conditions (Riste, Kahn, and Cruickshank 2001).

Another important theme globally is the massive migration around the world from rural to urban centers. In China, this influx has contributed to the largest migration in human history. The distinction between rural and urban populations is relevant not only in developing but also in developed countries. As we have seen, limited access to healthcare and proper diets has contributed to epidemic rates of diabetes in rural indigenous populations in North America. All major socioeconomic factors that affect diabetes can be seen at work in the difference between these two populations and the pressure, global in scope, to relocate from rural to urban environments. Although many in rural communities are at greater risk of not receiving adequate healthcare, a World Health Organization study has shown that, apart from China, all regions had at least as many cases in urban as in rural areas in 1995. This same report has shown that, by 2025, there will be a considerable excess of diabetes in the urban areas. For developing countries as a whole, the urban/rural ratio in diabetes frequency is predicted to rise from 1.6 in 1995 to 3.3 in 2025 (Wild et al. 2004).

In conclusion, the rates of diabetes and the social and economic impact of the disease are growing in every country in the world. Without sustained and cooperative education and government outreach, the prevalence of diabetes will reach epidemic proportions by 2025.

All medical and humanitarian sectors in addition to promoting education and preventative measures are also exploring new and innovative treatments. We will look at some of these new developments and potential therapies in Chapter 6.

6

The Future of Diabetes

As we have seen clearly in Chapter 5, the world health community and citizens from every nation face a mounting threat posed by diabetes. Cases of both type 1 and type 2 diabetes are growing in developing and developed countries on every continent. The costs of this rising epidemic are staggering, and there is real pressure on international, national, and local organizations to create viable solutions. In this chapter, we will focus on some of the future treatments being explored and learn more about the many exciting advances in diabetic care. The range of new developments is broad, and this chapter will look at innovations in science and pharmacology as well as new public health initiatives. In addition, we will look at the structure for scientific research used in the clinical studies being conducted by governments, universities, and drug makers (Personal Health Zone 2005).

Because of the epidemic rise in diabetes around the world, there are many different kinds of clinical trials and research being conducted. Both the public and private sectors are pouring billions of dollars into a wide range of exciting treatments, many of which are already showing results. The most exciting area of diabetic research is in the area of new treatments. Although no cures are in sight, there are a variety of effective new drugs and protocols in trial stages and being approved by the Food and Drug Administration (FDA). In addition to new drug therapies, other treatments are also showing dramatic potential. These include gene therapies, pancreatic and islet cell transplants, and new methods of administering current treatments that are less invasive and more effective. In addition to these advances, there are also new radical surgeries such as gastric bypass that have been shown to dramatically reduce obesity and therefore help in reducing the risk of type 2 adult-onset diabetes. Finally, there are also new advances in nutrition, including fat-free foods and more aggressive public awareness campaigns, both of which are vital tools in combating obesity and other risk factors.

FDA APPROVAL OF NEW DRUGS

Today, short of a miracle cure, the most promising treatments for both type 1 and type 2 diabetes continues to be different combinations of drug treatment, lifestyle changes, innovative methods of administering treatment, and surgery. Of these, drugs and surgery offer the most immediate and long-term effects for seriously ill patients. We will look first at innovations in drug therapies and later explore more radical solutions such as the full suite of surgery and transplants options being developed today.

Since 1990, more than ten new drugs have been approved for the treatment of diabetes, and there are currently 113 clinical trials on new treatment approaches listed with the FDA. The level of research and development in the field of diabetes has grown dramatically during the past decade, and, between 1995 and 2000, the number of new trials resulting in new therapies exceeded the total number of drugs released in the United States in the preceding half century (Leichter 2001).

One of the most important aspects of research and development in new treatments is clinical trials. Clinical trials accomplish two things. First, they allow for development of effective new drugs. Second, they are part of the approval process required by the FDA. The FDA is charged with protecting the public health by ensuring the safety, efficacy, and security of human and veterinary drugs, biological products, and medical devices. In addition, the FDA is also responsible for advancing public health by promoting research and development of newer and safer medicines. To do this, they have established a rigorous protocol for testing and approving experimental drugs. This process is called the New Drug Development and Review Process.

Getting a new drug approved for use by the general population is not easy. The FDA estimates that, on average, it takes more than eight years to research, test, and bring a drug to market, and many compounds are never approved. In addition to time, the costs are very high. Pharmaceutical companies spend millions every year developing and testing new compounds.

New drug research starts with a study of how the body functions and focuses on a particular disease or pathology. The researcher then conducts a series of test tube experiments called assays, in which individual compounds are added systematically to different enzymes, cell cultures, or cellular substances. The goal of these exhaustive experiments is to isolate compounds that indicate a chemical structure that may prove therapeutic. Researchers today rely heavily on computers to conduct much of this initial work modeling different compounds, receptor sites, and how different enzymes might behave. Once a promising compound has been isolated, the substance must be tested on a living being (usually an animal).

Once a compound has been discovered and preliminary tests have been conducted, a drug maker is ready to approach the FDA to begin the approval process. The first stage is preclinical research. In this stage, a company must submit data describing the drug, proof of its general safety, and the initial clinical studies that have been conducted to substantiate its review. Sometimes these data will come from other countries where the drug has already been approved. In this stage, the drug's developer will conduct laboratory tests on animals to evaluate the compounds toxicity and pharmacological effects. Other tests will evaluate how well the drug is metabolized and the rate at which the body excretes the compounds. These trials typically take from two weeks to three months.

Once preclinical trials have taken place, the drug maker is ready for phase 1 clinical trials on human subjects. These initial trials are sometimes conducted on patients, but more often healthy volunteers are used. The trials are designed to test the metabolic impact of the experimental drug, its side effects, and, of course, whether there are signs of effective therapeutic action. On average, the first phase of clinical trials will include twenty to eighty subjects.

Once sufficient information has been recorded from the phase 1 trials, and barring any toxicity reports that might disqualify the new drug, phase 2 studies begin. Phase 2 studies strive to be more tightly controlled and monitored than the preceding trials and typically are conducted on patients instead of volunteers. The researchers continue to test for toxicity and side effects associated with drug. The number of patients in a phase 2 control group usually involves several hundred.

In phase 3 studies, once the basic effectiveness of the drug has been established, the research is expanded to include both controlled and uncontrolled trials. In phase 3, the goal is to evaluate the overall benefit-risk relationship of the drug and to gather enough information to better establish the effectiveness of the drug. This information is intended both to support the efficacy of the drug and for labeling and protocols that will be communicated to physicians once the drug is approved. After phase 3, the drug maker is finally ready to submit their findings and appeal for approval to the FDA for review (Food and Drug Administration 2007b).

In addition to a surge in newly developed and approved drugs, clinical studies have shown that treatment for diabetes is often more effective when a combinations of drugs are used. Because of this, increasing emphasis has been placed on creating drug "cocktails" in which multiple therapies are combined. This combination therapy has, in turn, meant that new products will be judged not only for their effectiveness when used alone but also for their utility in combination with other therapies. This new approach has vastly increased the options available to healthcare providers and given them an opportunity for better clinical results through more treatment options. One complicating factor of this approach is that the complexity of mixing drugs makes the clinical decision-making process exponentially more difficult and expands the possibility of clinical error in designing different treatments. It also increases the difficulty of finding appropriate solutions from a social and economic point of view because, obviously, the more drugs one takes, the more expenses they incur.

PHARMACEUTICALS AVAILABLE TODAY

Today all diabetes pills sold in the United States are organized into five classes. These five classes of drugs are sulfonylureas, meglitinides, biguanides, TZDs, and alpha-glucosidase inhibitors. All five classes work in different ways to lower blood glucose levels.

Sulfonylureas and meglitinides both stimulate the beta cells of the pancreas to release more insulin. Sulfonylurea drugs are an older class of drugs that have been in use since the 1950s. Sulfonylureas are generally taken one to two times a day before meals; meglitinides are taken before every meal. Because sulfonylureas and meglitinides stimulate the release of insulin, some patients can develop hypoglycemia when taking them.

Biguanides lower blood glucose levels primarily by decreasing the amount of glucose produced by the liver. They also can help to lower blood glucose levels by making muscle tissue more sensitive to insulin, which allows glucose to be absorbed more effectively (American Diabetes Association 2007).

Rosiglitazone (Avandia), troglitazone (Rezulin), and pioglitazone (ACTOS) form a group of drugs called TZDs. These drugs help insulin work better in the muscle and fat and also reduce glucose production in the liver. The TZDs not only improve insulin sensitivity and glycemic control with reduced insulin requirements but also have potentially favorable effects on other components of a diabetic's metabolism. These beneficial effects on lipid metabolism, blood pressure, vascular tone, and endothelial function might directly and indirectly influence reduce cardiovascular risk by altering several pro-atherogenic metabolic processes and slowing the progression of premature cardiovascular disease (Mudaliar 2007).

TZDs are taken once or twice a day with food. Although effective in lowering blood glucose levels, TZDs can have a rare but serious effect on the liver. Additional studies and careful use of TZDs are necessary to ensure a better understanding of its role in the drug arsenal of diabetics and to limit any dangerous side effects (Karter et al. 2004).

The last class of drugs is Acarbose or alpha-glucosidase inhibitors. These are a class of drugs that help the body to lower blood glucose levels by blocking the breakdown of starches, such as bread, potatoes, and pasta in the intestine. This class of drugs also slows the breakdown of some sugars, such as table sugar, as well as staunches the rise in blood glucose levels after a meal. They should be taken with the first bite of a meal. The alpha-glucosidase inhibitors may include side effects such as gas and diarrhea.

In addition to the original five classes of drugs, there is a new class called Exenatide. Exenatide is the first new drug to emerge from an area of research that is focusing on hormones in the human intestine called incretin mimetics. This research looks at how these hormones impact digestion and how digestion in turn affects diabetes and weight. The hormones in the intestine are commonly referred to as gut hormones because they simulate insulin secretion. A key hormone produced in the human intestine is GLP-1. It stimulates insulin production without causing the symptoms of hypoglycemia and weight gain associated with insulin injections and some oral anti-diabetes agents. Research has focused on GLP-1 and has shown that it regulates the proliferation of insulin-manufacturing islet cells in the pancreas, a process that encourages the body to make more insulin-producing beta cells.

Currently, there are two incretin families. Exanetide (also known as Byetta) and Liraglutide are GLP-1 analogs. This means that they mimic the insulin-boosting effects of natural GLP-1, which typically diminishes the longer a person has diabetes.

The second family are dipeptidyl peptidase 4 (DPP4) inhibitors. This group was developed because the GLP-1 analogs must be given by injection. Because so many diabetics prefer oral admission, the DPP4 inhibitors were developed. Because the enzyme DPP4 quickly degrades natural GLP-1, DPP4 inhibitors are designed to block this process. The drugs in this group currently in development are called Januvia and Galvus; both inhibit DPP4, thus increasing natural GLP-1. Another advantage to the DDP4 inhibitors is that they are administered orally. In clinical trials, Januvia taken once a day increased the postprandial rise in active GLP-1 concentrations without causing hypoglycemia. The FDA has recently approved Januvia for use both as a monotherapy and in combination with TZDs.

One of the things that is most unique about the Exanetide class of drugs and that has been covered extensively in the media is its origin. Exenatide is a synthetic version of exendin-4, a hormone in the saliva of the Gila monster! The Gila monster is a lizard native to several southwestern American states. The hormone in the lizard's saliva displays properties similar to human GLP-1. What is so unique about the Gila lizard is its eating habits. The lizard eats only four times a year and turns its pancreas off the rest of the time. When it eats, it secretes exendin-4 to turn its pancreas on again (American Diabetes Association 2004).

Exenatide has been shown to be especially effective at regulating glycemic levels after meals. The period after a meal is referred to by healthcare practitioners and researchers as post-prandial. It is now well known that meal-stimulated circulating levels of GLP-1 are reduced in type 2 diabetes. Knowing this, researchers have focused on using a GLP-1 surrogate as a therapeutic agent in patients. Although Exenatide may lower blood glucose levels on its own, it can also be combined with other medications such as pioglitazone, metformin, sulfonylureas, and/or insulin to improve glucose control. The medication is injected twice per day using a prefilled pen device similar to those used in the administration of insulin. Clinical trials have shown that patient responses to Exenatide includes improvements in their initial rapid release of endogenous insulin, suppression of glucagon release by the pancreas, regulation of gastric emptying, and reduced appetite. All of these responses help to lower blood glucose.

Despite the effectiveness of the Exenatide class of drugs, as with all of diabetes care, these positive effects depend on the patient's understanding of the proper technique and timing of administration and their disciplined compliance with the regimen. It is important to remember that no diabetic drug can be effective unless a patient follows the proper testing and administering protocols (Triplitt and Chiquette 2006).

Another new drug recently approved for general use is called Pramlintide. Pramlintide does not involve GLP-1 like Exenatide and the DPP4 inhibitors. Instead, Pramlintide is an analog of a different gut hormone called Amylin. Despite its difference, like Exenatide, Pramlintide has been developed to regulate glucose actions in humans by slowing gastric emptying and suppressing glucagon secretion during the prandial/postprandial period. These actions, in conjunction with those of insulin, help reduce fluctuations in circulating glucose levels to a greater degree than is possible with insulin treatment alone.

The combined improvement of glycemic and weight control makes Pramlintide an effective compliment to insulin therapy and a potentially useful treatment option in overweight and obese patients with type 2 diabetes. Pramlintide is currently approved for use in the United States as a treatment for patients with type 1 and type 2 diabetes who have been unable to achieve desired glucose control despite insulin therapy (Buse, Weyer, and Maggs 2002).

In addition to the potential of regular daily doses of Exenatide, another drug, Exanetide LAR, has been developed to provide a longer-acting therapy. This preparation has been developed to be given only once a week. In a recent sixteen-week study, two doses of Exenatide LAR given once weekly were well tolerated and achieved dose-dependent improvements in glucose levels and overall body weight. Whether these beneficial effects of Exenatide LAR can be maintained in the longer term and, more importantly, whether it has effects on pancreatic B-cell regeneration in humans remains to be determined (Kim et al. 2007).

Another area of research that is the subject of intense clinical study is new quick-acting insulin analogs. These analogs, such as the recently developed drug Insulin Lispro, are biosynthetic forms of insulin that work because they are absorbed rapidly into a patient's circulation. By virtue of their more readily metabolized chemistry, insulin analogs have a more rapid onset of action than older soluble insulin preparations. They also have a shorter duration of action. Potential clinical benefits include better matching of peak insulin action to food absorption after meals and better glycemic control in the immediate postprandial period together with less risk of hypoglycemia in the period before the next meal is due. An important practical advantage for patients is that the insulin injection does not have to be taken thirty minutes before meals, as recommended for soluble insulin, but can be administered almost immediately before a meal (Feinglos et al. 1997). These faster-acting insulin analogs and long-acting insulin analogs such as Glargine are another vital step in the development of effective, safe, and easy to administer drugs for both type 1 and type 2 diabetics (Gale 1997).

As we have seen in previous chapters, the morbidity of diabetes is most often attributable to companion diseases that are enabled or exacerbated by the complications of diabetes. This is especially true of cardiovascular diseases and hypertension, which occurs in approximately thirty percent of patients with type 1 diabetes and fifty to eighty percent of patients with type 2 diabetes. Although the symptoms of hypertension are different for each type of diabetes, it dramatically increases the already high risk of cardiovascular and renal disease in both types. To combat hypertension, new anti-hypertensive drug treatments and ACEs have been developed. These drugs have been proven to prevent or delay kidney failure and have been shown to reduce cardiovascular morbidity and mortality. This success is in part attributable to the renoprotective effects of these two different drugs and their role in limiting the development and progression of diabetic renal disease (Landsberg and Molitch 2004).

The future continues to be bright for new drug therapies and research in ongoing. One final important consideration to bear in mind when thinking about drug therapies and their application in treating diabetes is the social and socioeconomic implication of aggressive treatment. One of the most important considerations, aside from side effects and general efficacy, is dosing frequency. In general, drug regimens that require fewer doses per day are associated with higher rates of compliance. This has been shown to be a pivotal component of proper maintenance of diabetes. Moreover, when it comes to oral hypoglycemic agents, drugs requiring more frequent doses per day are not necessarily more effective than those requiring fewer doses per day. The other consideration is, of course, cost. New therapies are expensive, and there continues to be a healthy debate about the overall cost-benefit analysis of new drugs vs. those treatments that are already well established (Leichter 2001).

NEW METHODS OF INSULIN DELIVERY

In addition to new oral and intravenous drug therapies, another important area of development in diabetes care is testing and drug delivery. One of the most visible aspects of diabetes, the testing and administering of insulin, is regularly listed by patients as one of the biggest inconveniences of the disease. Indeed, this is why there is so much emphasis on developing drugs that can be taken orally. The current regimen of glucose testing and insulin treatment is effective but limited by most diabetic's aversion to needles. Researchers continue to try and improve the method of testing and self-medication or administration of insulin as a way of both improving overall health as well as quality of life. The benefits of better testing and administration both help to improve the quality of life of diabetics as well as their compliance. It is well demonstrated that easier and less invasive methods of medication and testing markedly increase a patient's compliance with their daily regimen and that compliance dramatically improves overall health and control over diabetes. New advances and unorthodox methods of insulin delivery systems promise to improve this vital area.

One exciting new product is an inhaler similar to those used by asthmatics. Called an oral buccal system, it delivers a liquid aerosol formulation of insulin through a regularized dose inhaler (American Diabetes Association 2007).

One of the hopes for inhaled insulin is that it could free type 1 diabetic patients from frequent injections, although the administering of basal insulin will still require injections. The development of inhaled insulin is based on the technology used to deliver pulmonary medicine for respiratory diseases.

There are two major potential advantages of inhaled insulin. In addition to being less burdensome for the patient than intravenous delivery, research is also being conducted to chart how different types of insulin might be more successfully delivered using the inhalation method. Because different types of insulin work at different rates and for different amounts of time, different types of insulin are commonly known as short-acting, intermediate-acting, and long-acting Insulin. People with type 1 diabetes can often keep their glucose levels under control by taking shots of intermediate-acting or long-acting insulin in the morning or before bed, as well as taking shots of short-acting insulin before meals. However, although this type of routine has been shown to work for people with type 1 diabetes, many patients often stray from this routine, most likely because of the time requirements of taking so many shots. It is the time burden of intravenous administration that the inhaler can potentially address (American Diabetes Administration 2005b).

Although the use of insulin inhalers is still in trial stages, initial studies show that there are no long-term risks associated with pulmonary delivery, and the increased anti-insulin antibodies generated with inhaled insulin have been found not to adversely affect the availability or biologic activity of insulin (Nathan 2007).

In addition to pulmonary delivery, another advance that has already proven to be highly effective is insulin pumps. Insulin pumps can help some people achieve better control, and many people prefer this continuous system of insulin delivery over injections. Insulin pumps are computerized devices about the size of a cell phone that a patient can easily put in their pocket or clip to their belt. The pump delivers a steady, measured dose of insulin (the basal dose) through a flexible plastic tube called a catheter. The catheter is inserted through the skin into the patient's fatty tissue and is taped in place. In the most recent designs, the needle is removed and only a soft catheter remains implanted in the patient.

If the patient is using rapid-acting insulin, such as Humalog or Novalog, the pump can be programmed to release, on command, a bolus dose close to mealtime. This bolus dose helps regulate the rise in blood glucose that occurs after a meal. If the patient uses regular insulin, they would take the bolus dose about thirty minutes before mealtime.

The way a pump delivery system works is very simple: it closely mimics the body's normal release of insulin because it releases very small doses of insulin continuously just as a healthy pancreas would. Another important aspect of a pump is that they deliver very precise insulin doses at different times of the day. This regular precision dosing is necessary to correct for situations like the "dawn phenomenon" (the rise of blood glucose that occurs in the hours before and after waking; American Diabetes Association 2007).

Many diabetics choose the insulin pump because it enables them to enjoy a more flexible lifestyle and reduces both the responsibility and social stigma of testing. To use a pump, however, the patient must still fulfill many of the same responsibilities as before, such as checking their blood glucose frequently and learning how to make adjustments in insulin, food, and physical activity in response to those test results (see Figure 6.1).

One of the socioeconomic disadvantages of the pump is its cost. The pump typically carries an initial cost of $6,000–7,000 in addition to nearly $3,000 in yearly supplies (Haardt et al. 1994). Fortunately, most major insurance companies and Medicare now cover the pump. In addition, it has been conclusively shown that the cost-benefit analysis of adequate prevention, including the costs of emergency department visits attributable to problems with a patient's glucose regulation, support the pump. Another disadvantage is that first-time

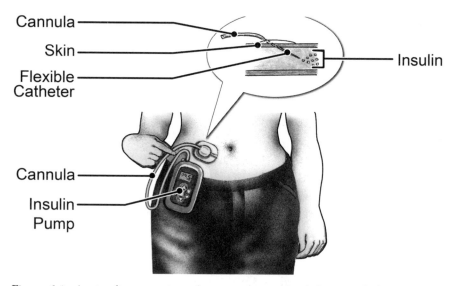

Figure 6.1. An insulin pump is used as a treatment for diabetes and eliminates the need for multiple injections throughout the day. The insulin pump can be worn on a belt strap much like a beeper. A catheter is placed under the skin and releases a bolus of insulin, which is stored in a cartridge located in the pump. The catheter must be changed every two to three days. *Illustration courtesy of Michael Brookman.*

users of the pump must be trained to use it safely and must make regular visits to their clinic to monitor its proper functioning. Despite these disadvantages, most patients feel that those inconveniences pale compared with the increase in flexibility and peace of mind provided by the pump.

Although pumps are an excellent alternative to conventional insulin therapy, they are only suited for specific subgroups of patients, for example, patients with recurrent severe hypoglycemia. Other advances promise new and exciting options. One is the development of an implantable artificial pancreas. The successful development of this device is linked to progress in the field of reliable long-duration glucose sensors. Another related device that is in development is a programmable implantable insulin pump. This is the most promising alternative to intensive subcutaneous insulin strategies or surgery in the short term, although researchers and engineers must still improve their safety and efficiency before they will be approved for general use (Selam and Charles 1990).

Another barrier researchers face in their search for alternatives to subcutaneous delivery of insulin is literally the skin of the patient. The permeability of the epidermal layer remains one of the greatest barriers to introducing insulin into a patient's body. A key concern is the effectiveness of the delivery system vis-à-vis the amount of insulin administered. Recent advances and research have included trials that use new technologies such as intranasal and the oral delivery systems discussed above (Cefalu 2004). Other innovative techniques to weaken the epidural layer currently in development include chemical substances, ultrasound techniques, and electrical current.

One of these techniques, called a jet injector, is a device that administers insulin without needles by delivering a high-pressure stream of insulin into subcutaneous tissue. Other systems being tested include iontophoresis, or low-frequency ultrasound. Iontophoresis refers to the concept of achieving transdermal delivery of insulin by direct electric current. A familiar example of this kind of technology is the transdermal medication patches that are currently being used to deliver nicotine for smoking cessation programs or hormone therapy for postmenopausal women. Iontophoresis is different from these patches because it uses a low-level electrical current, improving the delivery of the drug through the skin and into the surrounding tissue (Cefalu 2004). Low-frequency ultrasound is another method that has been shown to increase the permeability of the epidural layer to macromolecular drugs. This method is still in the research stage, however, and studies remain inconclusive. Furthermore, the insulin delivery rate via ultrasound may not provide for adequate physiological replacement.

The last major new delivery system currently in development is the pulmonary delivery, which we have already discussed. It is this method that shows signs of being the first approved alternative to insulin injections. The success of pulmonary delivered insulin therapy is largely attributable to the anatomic advantages of the lungs. The lungs provide an expansive and absorptive surface that is an optimal environment for drug absorption. In addition, the lungs do not have the same peptidases that are present in the gastrointestinal tract and that cause the degradation of absorbed insulin. Equally important, the lungs allow for a rapid onset of action after inhalation, and studies have shown that, after inhalation, insulin is rapidly absorbed with peak plasma concentrations being reached after fifteen to forty minutes. Another advantage is that the rapid absorption of inhaled insulin make it appropriate for use right before meals (White and Campbell 2001).

To date, all of the experimental approaches besides pulmonary delivery are still limited by the amount of insulin needed to effectively treat the patient, what is known as bioavailability. In other words, most alternatives to subcutaneous injection have proven unable to deliver enough drugs in an effective manner. So, for example, intranasal insulin treatment (administered through the nose like a nasal spray) is currently not an effective alternative to subcutaneous insulin because of its low bioavailability and high rate of treatment failure.

MODERN MONITORING

In addition to insulin pumps, there have been significant advances in the insulin monitoring equipment that are a constant companion in the lives of type 1 diabetics. The primary focus of new engineering in monitoring systems is the design of a device that allows for testing to be done in alternative places on the body such as the upper arm, forearm, base of the thumb, and thigh. Historically, monitoring has taken place by drawing blood from the patient's fingertips. The fingertips have been used because glucose readings have been found to be most reliable at the fingertip. In addition to generally being more reliable, the fingertip has also been shown conclusively to be the site that most quickly registers changes in glucose concentrations after a meal or administering medication. Although research is still ongoing, alternative sites have been shown to change more slowly than in the region of the fingertip. The FDA has ordered manufacturers to either demonstrate that their devices are not affected by differences between alternative site and fingertip blood samples during times of rapidly changing glucose or to educate users about the possibility of differing values at those important times.

One of the promising new monitoring systems recently approved by the FDA is the STS-7 Continuous Glucose Monitoring System manufactured by DexCom. The STS-7 is a device that works through a glucose sensor directly inserted right below the patient's skin on the abdomen. Once in place, the sensor uses an attached wireless transmitter. This transmitter is in turn calibrated using traditional finger-prick testing (Food and Drug Administration 2007a). Worn on the belt like a cell phone, the transmitter reports glucose values every five minutes for up to seven days before a new sensor must be inserted.

In addition to its convenience and the reduced discomfort of finger-prick testing, the approach known as "continuous monitoring" is able to produce regular readings that can, in turn, be used to detect trends and monitor patterns in a patient's glucose levels. With this additional information, both the patient and their healthcare provider can more effectively manage their diabetes as well as strategize about better long-term managed care solutions.

Despite the huge advances in mobility, all of the current advanced glucose monitoring systems still have one major limitation: they are not designed to replace a traditional blood glucose meter. Systems such as the STS-7 must still be used in conjunction with a traditional blood glucose meter to ensure a proper monitoring of the patient's health. What this means is that the added value of greater mobility is checked by the need to calibrate with a traditional monitoring device every twelve hours (Food and Drug Administration 2007a).

Another major limitation of the current class of new monitoring devices is that they are still subcutaneously inserted devices. As we have seen, diabetics are always calling for new technologies that reduce or even eliminate the need for needles. Because this is such a primary concern for diabetics, researchers continue to explore new technologies for glucose testing that avoids needles entirely. One of these uses a technology called near-infrared spectroscopy to measure glucose levels. Near-infrared spectroscopy measures glucose by shining a beam of light on the skin (Wozniak et al. 1999).

The FDA has approved one "minimally invasive" meter and one "noninvasive" glucose meter that use near-infrared spectroscopy. Unfortunately, neither of these two preliminary models is effective enough to warrant the elimination of standard glucose testing and can only be used to obtain glucose values between finger-prick tests. In addition, these devices require daily calibration using standard finger-prick glucose measurements.

Another new advancement in monitoring systems is the Cygnus Gluco-Watch Biographer. The GlucoWatch is worn on the arm like a wristwatch. It works by pulling tiny amounts of fluid from the skin and measuring their glucose levels. This is a noninvasive system that can provide up to three glucose measurements per hour for twelve hours. In addition to being noninvasive, the GlucoWatch has the added benefit of displaying results that can be read by the wearer as if they were looking at the time. At the current time, the

GlucoWatch's readings are not meant to be used as replacements for finger-prick-based tests. As with the other continuous monitoring systems, the regular testing results are meant to show trends and patterns in glucose levels rather than report any one result alone. This ability to monitor trends throughout the day is useful for detecting and evaluating episodes of hyperglycemia and hypoglycemia and determining their causes (Food and Drug Administration 2005).

Despite the ongoing limitations of all of the current alternatives to glucose monitoring systems, researchers continue to push the boundaries of technology and noninvasive solutions for insulin management. In the meantime, as we have seen, the data provided by these continuous monitoring systems can help patients identify trends in their disease. The trends include periods of previously hidden or undetectable nocturnal hypoglycemia and postprandial hyperglycemia. This new information is helpful for both researchers and patients, and current trials suggest that patient groups with both type 1 and type 2 diabetes that use continuous glucose monitoring system data to make adjustments in their regimen can achieve an overall reduction of blood glucose values and a drop in the frequency of glycemic episodes. In addition to better health, there is substantial evidence to suggest that more consistent glycemic control with continuous glucose monitoring can reduce the costs of healthcare to both the patient and the insurance provider (Mudaliar 2007).

TRANSPLANTS

In addition to the new drug therapies and delivery systems already discussed, surgery is the most exciting, effective, and potentially life-changing treatment for diabetes. Of course, there are risks and side effects to invasive surgical procedures that must be considered and can sometimes be dangerous. That being said, surgery is increasingly being used as an effective method of dealing with both type 1 and type 2 diabetes.

Right now, the closest thing to a cure for type 1 diabetes is a pancreas transplant. This kind of surgery is very risky and comes with a long list of complications. The first is the long wait to find a suitable donor. As with all transplant surgeries, there is a severe shortfall of suitable people who have elected to donate their organs after their own death. Despite the risks and obstacles to transplant surgery, each year approximately 1,300 people with type 1 diabetes receive whole-organ pancreas transplants. Studies show that, after one year, 83 percent of these patients, on average, have no symptoms of diabetes and do not have to take insulin to maintain normal glucose concentrations in the blood (National Institutes of Health 2007).

The major complication of transplant surgery is that patients who receive a transplanted organ must take powerful immunosuppressant medicines for the rest of their lives. These medications prevent the patient's body from rejecting the transplant and must be administered on a very strict schedule. If the patient stops taking these medicines, their body's immune system will recognize the new pancreas as a "stranger" and reject it. Because immunosuppressant drugs have a variety of serious side effects, including kidney failure, increased blood cholesterol levels, decreased white blood cell counts, and increased susceptibility to bacterial and viral infections, a physician must assess whether the health complications of taking these immune suppressants outweighs the benefits of the transplant. Because of the serious risks involved, pancreatic transplantation is typically only for individuals with end-stage renal disease or those with severe metabolic complications for whom the benefits outweigh the risks of a serious surgical procedure and a lifetime of immunosuppression (National Institutes of Health 2007). At this stage, pancreatic transplants are not suitable for children and adolescents. Instead, recent advances in immunosuppressive therapy and transplant biology have enabled younger patients and those with less severe symptoms of type 1 diabetes to receive islet cell transplantation.

One of the primary goals of medical researchers is to develop a way for people with type 1 diabetes to live without daily insulin injections. The most promising area of research in this area is an experimental procedure called islet cell transplantation. In islet transplantation, islets cells are taken from a donor pancreas (currently these are taken from cadavers) and transferred into a person with type 1 diabetes. Once implanted, the beta cells in these islets begin to make and release insulin.

Scientists have made many advances in islet transplantation in recent years. The first major breakthrough is known as the Edmonton Protocol. This trial's findings, reported in the June 2000 issue of the *New England Journal of Medicine*, described the work done by researchers at the University of Alberta in Edmonton, Canada.

The Edmonton study showed very promising results from islet transplantation in seven patients with type 1 diabetes. In their published findings, all seven patients in the study who had received the islet transplant remained free of insulin injections up to fourteen months after the procedure (Personal Health Zone 2005).

In the 2005 annual report of the Collaborative Islet Transplant Registry, it was reported that, after one year, 58 percent of those who had transplants no longer needed to inject insulin. For those who were still insulin-dependent one year after islet cell transplantation (33 percent of the patients followed by the registry) requirements for insulin were decreased. The average reduction in insulin requirements was 69 percent. The report concluded with the impressive statistic that 91 percent of those patients who underwent islet cell transplants showed improvement after the procedure.

The goal of islet transplantation is to infuse enough islets to control the blood glucose level without insulin injections. For an average-sized person (154 pounds), a typical transplant requires about one million islets, extracted from two donor pancreases. Unfortunately, like with pancreatic transplants, patients need to take immunosuppressive drugs to stop the immune system from rejecting the transplanted islets (National Institutes of Health 2007).

The results of the Edmonton protocol are very encouraging, but unfortunately, recent studies have reported that the rate of insulin independence five years after transplantation is as low as 10 percent. Another setback is the lack of availability of islet cells, which must come from a deceased person. Only about 6,000 pancreases a year become available for transplantation or for harvesting of islets. To avoid this problem, researchers are pursuing alternative sources, such as creating islets from other types of cells. New technologies could then be used to grow islets in the laboratory. The struggle to create islet cells can be seen in light of the larger effort to obtain stem cells. Stem cells have been widely reported in the news as being both potentially very helpful in fighting a range of diseases and for being controversial. The controversy surrounds the source of stem cells, which to date is primarily tissue taken from fetal tissue, a process that kills the fetus and that many see as immoral and akin to abortion. New research is currently underway to find alternative sources of stem cells that are not as morally controversial (National Diabetes Information Clearinghouse 2006).

Concerted efforts are underway in laboratories worldwide to develop alternative sources and strategies to obtain, propagate, and protect transplanted islet cells. These efforts include techniques to encapsulate islet xenografts, exploiting the burgeoning science of embryonic stem cell biology and isolating and propagating islet cell progenitor cells from adult pancreas or extra-pancreatic sources (American Diabetes Association 2007).

STEMMING OUT TO STEM CELL RESEARCH

Since the discovery of stem cells, teams of researchers have also been investigating the possibility that human embryonic stem cells could be developed as a therapy for treating both type 1 and type 2 diabetes. Recent studies in mice show that embryonic stem cells can be coaxed into differentiating into insulin-producing beta cells, and new reports indicate that this strategy may also be possible using human embryonic cells. In theory, embryonic stem cells could be cultivated as insulin-producing islet cells of the pancreas. With a ready supply of cultured stem cells, researchers hope that a line of embryonic stem cells could be grown for patients who require a transplant. The cells could be engineered to avoid immune rejection. Before transplantation, these cells could be placed into nonimmunogenic materials, which would hopefully mean that they would not be rejected by the patient and they could hopefully avoid the effects of immunosuppressant drugs (National Institutes of Health 2007).

Other research shows that there is some evidence that cells derived from embryonic stem cells might be less likely to cause immune rejection. Although at this point the technology does not exist to supply insulin-producing cells for transplant into humans, research is promising. In addition, whereas some researchers are pursuing research on embryonic stem cells, there are others trials aimed at investigating insulin-producing precursor cells that occur naturally in adult and fetal tissues.

One new area of research that has shown significant initial promise is a small trial conducted in Brazil that used a patient's own stem cells to treat type 1 diabetes. This procedure involved stimulating the patients' bodies to produce new stem cells and harvesting them from the patient's blood, which was then followed by multiple treatments of high-dose chemotherapy. The purpose of the chemotherapy was to shut down the patient's immune system and stop destruction of the few remaining insulin-producing cells in the body. Once the old cells are destroyed, the harvested stem cells were injected back into the body to build a new healthier immune system that did not attack the insulin-producing cells.

The results of the Brazil study were dramatic. The *New England Journal of Medicine* reported that, of the initial trial of fifteen patients with type 1 diabetes, all but one did not need insulin after the surgery. Although the results of the Brazil study are phenomenal, most researchers agree that the results must be repeated in a bigger study and with a proper control group. Another unique characteristic of the trial was that all the participating patients had been diagnosed with diabetes for less than six weeks. It remains to be seen whether the results can be reproduced in a larger and more diverse group of patients (ABC News Medical Unit 2007).

In all of the new treatments being explored using stem cells, there is controversy that surrounds their origin. One of the most important areas of research continues to be exploring alternative sources. For example, there continues to be controversy around whether adult stem cells exist in the pancreas and whether they could be harvested. There are some researchers who believe there are stem cell-like cells that can be found in the pancreatic ducts and even potentially in the islets themselves. Another camp maintains that ductal cells may be able to differentiate into islet precursor cells, whereas still another group of researchers argue that new islet cells arise from stem cells in the blood. Researchers are using several approaches for isolating and cultivating stem cells or islet precursor cells from fetal and adult pancreatic tissue to continue this vital area of research. In addition, several new promising studies indicate that insulin-producing cells can be cultivated from embryonic stem cell lines (National Institutes of Health 2001).

Before any cell-based therapy to treat diabetes is authorized for mainstream use, major safety concerns must be addressed. One serious issue is whether a precursor or stem-like cells transplanted into the body might induce the formation of tumors.

Ultimately, type 1 diabetes may prove to be especially difficult to cure because the cells are destroyed when the body's own immune system attacks and destroys them. It is the patient's own autoimmune response that must be solved if researchers hope to use transplanted cells to replace those that are damaged. For the time being, immunosuppressive therapies like those used in the Edmonton protocol hold the greatest promise. In theory, embryonic cells can be engineered to escape or reduce detection by the immune system.

Another method of avoiding detection is to encapsulate or embed islet cells derived from islet stem or progenitor cells in a material that would allow small molecules such as insulin to pass through freely but would not allow interactions between the islet cells and cells of the immune system. In this method, encapsulated cells could secrete insulin into the bloodstream but remain inaccessible to the immune system.

SURGICAL SOLUTIONS

Although the promise of transplantation is welcome news for type 1 diabetics, those suffering from type 2 diabetes have fewer options. As we have discussed, many type 2 diabetics are obese, and their BMI is a major component in their disease. For many obese type 2 diabetics, the most widely used surgical treatment available is either Lap-Band or gastric bypass. Both procedures are radical surgical interventions that help restrict the dietary intake of severely obese people, thereby helping them to lose weight. These procedures are primarily indicated for sufferers of type 2 diabetes whose condition will worsen exponentially if they do not lose weight and increase their mobility. An NIH Consensus Development Panel has recommended that patients with type 2 diabetes and with a BMI of 35 kg/m^2 consider this surgery (Franz et al. 2003).

The first of these two procedures to be developed and successfully used is known as gastric bypass. Gastric bypass is considered to be the most successful procedure in the surgical treatment of severe obesity, with greater than 50 percent of excess weight loss occurring within two years after the surgery. Although it was initially held to be risky, advances over the past five years has made this surgery safer and, as a result, a much more popular alternative for obese people. The process includes two procedures. The first redirects food by surgically bypassing most of the intestine. The second staples the stomach to dramatically reduces its size, allowing for no more than an ounce of food. The two procedures together both radically reduce the amount of food an individual can safely eat and, by reducing the length of time the food is in the digestive tract, minimizes the amount of calories that can be absorbed (Schneider and Mun 2005).

The greatest result of the surgery is not the initial weight reduction but the fact that, for a majority of those who undergo gastric bypass, the weight remains off even over many years. The clinical data are very clear about the beneficial effects of obesity surgery on glucose control and metabolic disorders in impaired glucose tolerant and type 2 diabetic subjects. An impressive 70–90 percent of diabetic patients remained euglycemic several years after the surgery. Professionals believe that the positive impact of gastric bypass surgery on glucose control results not only from significant weight loss but also from the exclusion of the hormonally active foregut, an area of diabetic research already covered above (Czupryniak 2004).

The second and newer surgical procedure is called Lap-Band. The name Lap-Band comes from the surgical technique used, which is laparoscopic, and the name of the implanted medical device that is called a gastric band. The Lap-Band System uses a silicone ring that is designed to be placed around the upper part of the stomach. Similar to the staples used in gastric bypass, the gastric band is designed to create a new, smaller stomach pouch that can hold only a limited amount of food (Schneider and Mun 2005). The basic principle of both systems is that, when a patient's stomach is smaller, they feel full faster. At the same time, the food moves more slowly between the upper and lower stomach as it is digested, and, as a result, the patient eats less and loses weight.

One related area to curbing obesity is in the area of modified nutrition, specifically the new fat-free foods being developed and marketed. There is a new burgeoning sector of commercially available foods that claim to be "fat free." Although it is true that avoiding saturated fats and other fattening foodstuffs is an important step in maintaining healthy nutrition and avoiding risk factors associated with diabetes, there are some commonly made mistakes. The first mistake is that very often consumers look at the amount of fat in a product and forget to focus on the amount of carbohydrates. The second is that use of fat substitutes such as Olestra is not necessarily a solution to avoiding a high-fat diet. In reasonable amounts (five low-fat or no-fat products per day), fat substitutes were responsible for a small decrease in dietary fat, saturated fat, and cholesterol intake with little or no decrease in total energy intake or weight. However, although fat substitutes can be helpful in small amounts, when they are used as a substantial substitution of daily nutrition, there can be a significant decrease in energy intake. This can have deleterious affects on the health of a diabetic. Long-term studies are still needed to determine the lasting effect of these new foods that contain fat replacers/substitutes (Franz et al. 2003).

One final and vital aspect of the overall fight against diabetes is clinical trials and research. As we have seen throughout this chapter, many different groups from pharmaceutical companies to nonprofit organizations and medical schools are all aligned to try and develop new advanced treatments. At the core of most of these groups is clinical research. Clinical research used medical trials and large control groups to investigate the efficacy of new treatments and study patterns in the different types of diabetes. One example of the way these groups can function is The Environmental Determinants of Diabetes in the Young (TEDDY) consortium. TEDDY is an international group of clinical centers whose goal is to identify infectious agents, dietary factors, or other environmental factors (including psychosocial events) that can trigger type 1 diabetes in those who are genetically susceptible. In addition, the consortium has committed itself to four basic strategies for fighting type 1 diabetes. The first is to create a central repository of data and biological samples for use by researchers. The second is to develop novel approaches to finding the causes of type 1 diabetes. The third is find ways to understand how the disease starts and progresses. The fourth is to discover new methods to prevent, delay, and reverse type 1 diabetes.

CLINICAL TRIALS

In addition to focusing on causes of diabetes and using clinical trials to investigate possible cures, TEDDY is concerned with highlighting the importance of different groups working together and sharing information. This importance is clearly demonstrated by the important groups who fund TEDDY, such as the NIDDK, the National Institute of Allergy and Infectious Diseases (NIAID), the National Institute of Child Health and Human Development, the National Institute of Environmental Health Sciences, the CDC, the

Juvenile Diabetes Research Foundation, and the ADA (National Institute of Diabetes and Digestive and Kidney Diseases 2005).

Another important research institute is the NIDDK. The NIAID is a branch of the NIH, and both conducts its own research and grants funds to other organizations (such as TEDDY). One of the important roles of the NIDDK is to maintain a clinical trials database, which serves as a clearing-house for new information, provides resources for researchers, and tracks trends in current clinical methods. The clinical research promoted by the NIDDK is designed to be patient oriented and conducted on human volunteers or on samples voluntarily given by human subjects. NIH-funded clinical studies are designed to answer specific medical questions. The NIH, like other important research institutions, advocates for safe and medically responsible clinical trials, believing that they are the fastest and best way to find improved treatments and preventions for diseases. Clinical trials or interventional trials are designed to ascertain whether different experimental preventions, treatments, or new ways of using known therapies are safe and effective under controlled conditions. In this way, the NIH is able to support and promote safe and aggressive cutting-edge research both nationally and around the world. Another vital resource is the website ClinicalTrials.gov, a government-sponsored site devoted to regularly updated information about federally and privately supported clinical research in human volunteers. ClinicalTrials.gov also provides information about the different purposes of clinical trials, who may participate, locations, and phone numbers for more details should a patient or researcher want to participate (National Library of Medicine 2007).

Another aspect of research and clinical trials that has become a vital part of community outreach and public health is gene screening. As we have seen in preceding chapters, education is a vitally important piece in the fight again diabetes. Gene screening can provide earlier detection for family members who may be at higher risk for developing diabetes. Researchers have shown one method of finding genes associated with increased risk of diabetes is by studying the whole genome, what is known as genome linkage studies. In this process, the entire genome of affected family members is scanned, and the families are followed over several generations and/or large numbers of affected sibling pairs are studied. By using such a broad clinical approach, researchers can search for associations between different parts of the genome and the risk of developing diabetes. Today, only two genes, calpain 10 (CAPN10) and hepatocyte nuclear factor 4 alpha (HNF4A), have been identified using linkage studies, but the research continues and many doctors are hopeful that, by promoting gene screening in at-risk communities, early intervention will dramatically reduce the number of people who contract type 2 (Winckler et al. 2005).

CONCLUSION

In conclusion, diabetes continues to grow as a major health epidemic and public health challenge. Despite growing populations, however, there are many reasons to feel optimistic. Progress in all fields of diabetes treatment is excellent, and major clinical trials continue to reveal new and exciting therapies. New drugs, implantable glucose sensors, and inhaled insulin are just a few of these exciting new treatments. In addition, major advances are taking place in stem cell and islet cell transplantation efforts in addition to radical surgeries, such as gastric bypass, that have proven to be extremely helpful in reducing obesity in type 2 diabetics. There also continues to be large-scale implementation of public health initiatives aimed at educating at risk populations. Only time will tell whether these new treatments and education initiatives will be able to control the ballooning cost both economically and socially of diabetes worldwide.

Timeline

1552 BC	The Ebers Papyrus, written in hieratic script, is the oldest and most complete medical record from ancient Egypt.
400 BC	Two of the most influential texts, including *Shushruta Samhita* and *Charaka Samhita*, make references to diabetes.
3rd Century BC	Apollonius Memphites authored a work titled *On the Names of the Parts of the Human Body*. The modern version of the Hippocratic Oath states, "I will remember that there is art to medicine as well as science, and that warmth, sympathy, and understanding may outweigh the surgeon's knife or the chemist's drug."
200 BC	Demetrios of Apameia described the word we know today: diabetes. Aretaeus states, "Diabetes is a dreadful affliction, not very frequent among men, being a melting down of the flesh and limbs into urine."
	Galen documented his medical knowledge in seventeen volumes, titled *On the Localisation of Diseases*.

The most prominent ancient Chinese physician, Chang Chung-Ching, writes *Treatise on Colds and Fevers*, describing diabetes as "clouding of the urine, frigidity, and swelling of the lower limbs."

9th Century   Rhazes suggests changes in nutritional regimens for treating various ailments, such as polyuria.

10th Century   Avicenna's writes his major literary work *Canon of Medicine*. This fourteen-volume text organized and explained disease processes along with recommendations for treatment.

12th Century   Maimonides is well known for his literary work *Fusul Musa*, which contained medical aphorisms on numerous subjects.

16th Century   Paracelsus believed that there was a link between medicine and the study of alchemy. He evaporated a liter of urine, and he recovered four ounces of what he thought was salt, although it was actually sugar.

17th Century   Willis "claimed that diabetes was primarily a disease of the blood and not the kidneys. Willis believed that the sweetness appeared first in the blood and was later found in the urine."

Dobson performed a series of experiments to prove that diabetes was, in fact, a disease affecting the bloodstream.

The term "diabetes mellitus" is coined by William Cullen.

1769   Cullen's *Synopsis Nosologiae Methodicae* describes differences between diabetes insipidus and diabetes mellitus.

18th Century   Rollo is responsible for the first nutritional approach to diabetes control.

19th Century   Claude Bernard found that sugar is formed in the liver and stored as glycogen.

1869   Paul Langerhans finds that the pancreas is made up of two distinct systems.

1889   Oskar Minkowski and Joseph von Mering unarguably link pancreatic function to diabetes by experimenting with dogs.

1909   Jean de Meyer first proposed the name "insula."

1921   Frederick Banting and his assistant Charles Best successfully isolate insulin from dog pancreases.

1922	Nicolae Paulescu published an article describing his successful isolation of insulin.
January 23, 1922	Insulin extracts first tested on a human being, a fourteen-year-old boy named Leonard Thompson, in Toronto, Canada (Canadian Diabetes Association).
October 25, 1923	Dr. Banting and Macleod are awarded the Nobel Prize in physiology (Canadian Diabetes Association).
1930s	Sulfonamides were developed by a German by the name of Gerhard Domagk.
1944	A standardized syringe was developed for the administration of insulin.
1946	Loubatières "concluded that sulfonamides exerted blood glucose-lowering effects by stimulating the pancreas to release insulin."
1955	Oral medications become available for the treatment of hyperglycemia.
1959	Two major types of diabetes are recognized: type 1 diabetes and type 2 diabetes (Canadian Diabetes Association).
1966	First transplant of a pancreas was performed.
1983	Humilin insulin is discovered.
1986	Insulin pens become available to the medical community.
1992	Experiments are conducted with a new form of insulin known as Lispro.
1993	The Diabetes Control and Complications Trial states that intense control of diabetic condition through therapy helps to reduce the chances of developing long-term complications.
1995	Metformin approved for use in type 2 diabetes.
1999	Researchers find that insulin is responsible for controlling the secretion of hormones from fat.
2001	Stem cells were found to take the form of insulin-producing cells. Low-fat diet and exercise was shown to reduce the chances of developing diabetes by half.

2006   The Food and Drug Administration approves the use of Januvia as an oral medication for the treatment of diabetes.

2007   Stem cell transplant of fifteen patients with new onset diabetes in a Brazilian study. Thirteen of these patients were able to stay off of insulin for a prolonged period of time.

Glossary

ACE inhibitor: Blood pressure medication used in diabetics to decrease the risk of developing kidney disease.

Acute: Within a short period of time.

Adult-onset diabetes: Term used to describe type 2 diabetes.

Alpha cell: A cell in the pancreas that secretes glucagon.

Antibody: Protects the body from foreign matter.

Atherosclerosis: A disease in which there is an increased deposition of fat particles on the walls of arteries.

Autoimmune disease: The body mistakenly mounts an immune attack against its own body parts.

Beta cell: A cell found in the pancreas that produces insulin.

Blood glucose: The main sugar of the body that is found in the bloodstream. It is a source of energy for cells.

Blood glucose meter: A device that measures the amount of glucose that is in the bloodstream at a given point in time.

Body mass index (BMI): A scale used to evaluate the gradation of size of a person using a ratio of weight and height.

Bunion: A large mass on the first joint of the great toe of the foot that can lead to infections.

Calorie: A unit of energy that comes from food.

Carbohydrate: Forms of sugars and starches that are ultimately broken down into glucose.

Certified diabetes educator: American Diabetes Association–trained professionals that teach diabetics how to manage the disease.

Clinical trial: A controlled study that determines the efficacy of a new treatment.

C-peptide: A useful test in establishing the amount of insulin secreted by the pancreas.

Diabetic ketoacidosis: A medical emergency that results from the buildup of ketone bodies in the bloodstream. Symptoms include nausea, vomiting, and coma.

Dialysis: A process in which blood is filtered by a machine that mimics the actions of the kidney.

DNA: Contains genetic material that houses information that is inherited by future generations.

Edema: Swelling or collection of fluids in cellular compartments.

Endocrine glands: Glandular tissue that releases substances known as hormones directly into the bloodstream.

End-stage renal disease: Disease in which the kidneys are nonfunctioning and require either dialysis or a transplant.

Enzyme: A protein that is found in the body that is involved in increasing the efficacy of chemical reactions.

Epidemiology: The study of a disease in regards to how many people are affected and how many new cases appear yearly.

Etiology: Study of the causes of disease.

Exogenous: Formed outside the body.

Fasting blood glucose test: Tests the amount of blood glucose usually in the morning before ingestion of a meal. A reading of 126 mg/dl or higher is diagnostic for diabetes.

Fat: Serves as a form of energy storage.

Fatty acid: Basic unit of fat; can be converted to energy by the body.

Gangrene: Tissue death that results from a decrease in blood flow.

Gestation: The length of time that a woman is pregnant.

Gestational diabetes mellitus: Diabetes that occurs during pregnancy, and blood glucose levels are elevated. Glucose usually normalizes after birth.

Glaucoma: Increased ocular pressure.

Glucagon: A hormone that is secreted by the alpha cells that increases the amount of glucose in the bloodstream.

Glucose: The main source of energy of the body.

Glucose tolerance test: A certain amount of glucose is ingested by the patient to see whether the person is able to tolerated a glucose load. Can be used to see whether the person has diabetes.

Glycogen: The main storage form of glucose.

Hormone: A chemical that is secreted by endocrine glands into the bloodstream.

Hyperglycemia: A state of elevated blood glucose that produce symptoms of thirst, dry mouth, and increased urination.

Hyperinsulinism: Increased levels of insulin in the bloodstream.

Hypoglycemia: Low levels of glucose in the blood.

Immunosuppressant: Something that decreases the bodies ability to mount an immune response.

Impotence: Inability to maintain an erection as a result of nerve or blood vessel damage.

Incidence: Frequency of occurrence of a disease.

Insulin: A hormone produced by the beta cells of the pancreas that is involved in the utilization of glucose by the cells of the body.

Insulin pen: An injection device that delivers insulin through a needle.

Insulin pump: Provides a continuous means of insulin administration through a flexible catheter that is inserted into the skin.

Insulin receptor: Found on the plasma membrane of the cell and is involved in joining with insulin to promote glucose entrance into the cell.

Insulin resistance: The loss of the ability of the cells to respond to the effects of insulin.

Jet injector: A high pressure delivery system of insulin.

Juvenile-onset diabetes: A term used to describe type 1 diabetes.

Ketone body: A breakdown product of fat attributable to low levels of insulin in the blood.

Kidneys: Organs that are found in the posterior portion of the abdominal cavity that are involved in filtering blood and forming urine.

Lancet: A sharp blade that is used to prick the skin to elicit blood.

Metabolism: The chemical conversion of food into energy to sustain life.

Metformin: Used in the treatment of type 2 diabetes.

Microalbuminuria: The finding of small amounts of albumin in the urine.

Nephropathy: A disease that causes damage to the vessels of the kidney, thereby impairing function.

Neuropathy: A disease that results in the destruction of nerves.

Obesity: A condition in which a person has an increased amount of fat in the body. Calculated as a BMI that is greater than 30.0.

Oral glycemic agents: Medication that is taken by mouth to decrease the levels of blood sugar in the body.

Pancreas: An organ with both endocrine and exocrine functions. The islets of Langerhans are involved in the control of insulin and glucose.

Peripheral vascular disease: Presents with aches in the legs and feet that are attributable to decreased function of the vasculature and impaired blood flow.

Polyuria: Increased urination.

Postprandial glucose: The level of glucose that is measured after the ingestion of a meal.

Somatostatin: Hormone produced by the delta cells of the pancreas that is involved in the control of insulin and glucagon.

Subcutaneous delivery: The injection of medicine under the skin.

Type 1 diabetes: A form of diabetes in which that pancreas makes little or no insulin and hyperglycemia results. Usually treated with insulin injections and is more common to a younger population.

Type 2 diabetes: A disease that is as a result of a resultant resistance to insulin that leads to hyperglycemia and hyperinsulinemia. Treated with diet, exercise, and oral medications.

Vein: A blood vessel that is involved in carrying blood toward the heart.

Bibliography

ABC News Medical Unit. 2007. "Stem Cells: A Possible Cure for Diabetes." April 10. Available at: http://abcnews.go.com/Health/Diabetes/Story?id=3026694&page=3.

American Diabetes Association. 2004. "First of New Class of Drugs for Diabetes Successful." Available at: http://www.diabetes.org/for-media/2004-press-releases/new-drug-class.jsp.

American Diabetes Association. 2005a. "Using the Diabetes Food Pyramid." Available at: http://www.diabetes.org/nutrition-and-recipes/nutrition/foodpyramid.jsp.

American Diabetes Association. 2005b. "Is Inhaled Insulin as Good as Insulin Shots?" Available at: http://www.diabetes.org/diabetes-research/summaries/skyler-inhaled-insulin.jsp.

American Diabetes Association. 2006. "Advocacy Goals: Action for 2006."Available at: http://www.diabetes.org/uedocuments/AdvocacyGoals2006.pdf.

American Diabetes Association. 2007. *Diabetes 4-1-1: Facts, Figures, and Statistics at a Glance.* Alexandria, VA: American Diabetes Association.

American Diabetes Association. N.d. "What Is Exercise?" Available at: http://www.diabetes.org/weightloss-and-exercise/exercise/what-is-exercise.jsp.

Anderson RA. 1997. "Chromium as an Essential Nutrient for Humans." *Regulatory Toxicology and Pharmacology* 26:S35–S41.

Anderson RA. 1998. "Chromium, Glucose Intolerance, and Diabetes." *Journal of the American College of Nutrition* 17:548–55.

Anderson RA. 2004. "Cinnamon Extracts Boost Insulin Sensitivity." *Agricultural Research* 48:21. Available at: http://www.ars.usda.gov/is/AR/archive/jul00/cinn0700.htm.

Aubrey A. 2006. "KFC Will Cut Trans Fat from Its Famous Recipe." National Public Radio.

Baird J. 2007. "Erectile Dysfunction." National Kidney and Urologic Diseases Information Clearinghouse, January 1.

Balk E, Tatsioni A, Lichtenstein A, Lau J, Pittas AG. 2007. "Effect of Chromium Supplementation on Glucose Metabolism and Lipids: A Systematic Review of Randomized Controlled Trials." *Diabetes Care*, published online, May 22. Available at: http://care.diabetesjournals.org/cgi/reprint/dc06-0996v1.

Barry JM. 2002. *Campbell's Urology*. 8th ed., vol. 1. Philadelphia: W. B. Saunders.

Bartter FC, Berkson BM, Gallelli J, Hiranaka P. 1980. "Treatment of Four Delayed-Mushroom-Poisoning Patients with Thioctic Acid." In Faulstich H, Kommerell B, Wieland T, eds., *Amanita Toxins and Poisonings*. Baden-Baden: Witzstrock.

Berkson BM. 1999. "A Conservative Triple Antioxidant Approach to the Treatment of Hepatitis C: Three Case Histories." *Medizinische Klinik* 94:84–89.

Bhatt DL, Topol EJ. 2002. "Need to Test the Arterial Inflammation Hypothesis." *Circulation* 106:136–40.

Bliss M. 1982. *The Discovery of Insulin*. Chicago: University of Chicago Press.

Brautigan DL, Kruszewski A, Wang H. 2006. "Chromium and Vanadate Combination Increases Insulin-Induced Glucose Uptake by 3T3-L1 Adipocytes." *Biochemical and Biophysical Research Communications* 347:769–73.

Briscoe VJ, Davis SN. 2006. "Hypoglycemia in Type 1 and Type 2 Diabetes: Physiology, Pathophysiology, and Management." *Clinical Diabetes* 24:115–21.

Buse JB, Weyer C, Maggs DG. 2002. "Amylin Replacement with Pramlintide in Type 1 and Type 2 Diabetes: A Physiological Approach to Overcome Barriers with Insulin Therapy." *Clinical Diabetes* 20:137–44.

Butler AE, Janson J, Bonner-Weir S, Ritzel R, Rizza RA, Butler PC. 2003. "β-Cell Deficit and Increased β-Cell Apoptosis in Humans with Type 2 Diabetes." *Diabetes* 52:102–10.

Callahan TL, Caughey AB. 2006. *Blueprints Obstetrics and Gynecology*. Philadelphia: Lippincott Williams & Wilkins.

Cefalu WT. 2004. "Concept, Strategies, and Feasibility of Noninvasive Insulin Delivery." *Diabetes Care* 27:239–46.

Clark N. 2003. "The Debate Continues: Setting the Record Straight about Carbs and Protein." *Nutrition American Fitness*, May–June.

Costanzo LS. 2006. *Physiology*. 3rd ed. Philadelphia: Saunders Elsevier.

Czupryniak L. 2004. "Gastric Bypass Surgery in Severely Obese Type 1 Diabetic Patients." *Diabetes Care* 27:2561–62.

Davidson MB. 2003. "The Case for 'Outsourcing' Diabetes Care." *Diabetes Care* 26:1608–12.

Dick M. 1998. *The Ancient Ayurvedic Writings*. Available at: http://www.ayurveda.com/online%20resource/ancient_writings.htm.

Dionne SI. 2002. "Urinary System." In Krapp K, ed., *Encyclopedia of Nursing and Allied Health*. Farmington Hills, MI: Gale Group.

Edelstein L. 1943. *From the Hippocratic Oath: Text, Translation, and Interpretation*. Baltimore: Johns Hopkins University Press.

Feinglos MN, Thacker CH, English J, Bethel MA, Lane JD. 1997. "Modification of Postprandial Hyperglycemia with Insulin Lispro Improves Glucose Control in Patients with Type 2 diabetes." *Diabetes Care* 20:1539–42.

Feld L. 2006. "Renal Glucosuria." Available at: http://www.emedicine.com/ped/topic1991.htm#section~author_information.

Food and Drug Administration. 2005. "Glucose Meters and Diabetes Management." Available at: http://www.fda.gov/diabetes/glucose.html#11.

Food and Drug Administration. 2007a. "STS-7 Continuous Glucose Monitoring System—P050012/S001." Available at: http://www.fda.gov/cdrh/mda/docs/P050012S001.html.

Food and Drug Administration. 2007b. "The New Drug Development Process." Available at: http://www.fda.gov/cder/handbook/develop.htm.

Foster TS. 2007. "Efficacy and Safety of α-Lipoic Acid Supplementation in the Treatment of Symptomatic Diabetic Neuropathy." *Diabetes Educator* 33:111–17.

Franz MJ, Bantle JP, Beebe CA, Brunzell JD, Chiasson JL, Garg A, Holzmeister LA, Hoogwerf B, Mayer-Davis E, Mooradian AD, Parnell JQ, Wheeler M; American Diabetes Association. 2003. "Evidence-Based Nutrition Principles and Recommendations for the Treatment and Prevention of Diabetes and Related Complications." *Diabetes Care* 26:S51–S61.

Frazier L. 2007. "Fighting Diabetes Naturally." Available at: http://www.natural productsmarketplace.com/articles/fighting-diabetes-naturally.html.

Furukawa Y. 1999. "Enhancement of Glucose-Induced Insulin Secretion and Modification of Glucose Metabolism by Biotin." *Nippon Rinsho* 57:2261–69.

Gabriely I, Wozniak R, Mevorach M, Kaplan J, Aharon Y, Shamoon H. 1999. "Transcutaneous Glucose Measurement Using Near-Infrared Spectroscopy during Hypoglycemia." *Diabetes Care* 22:2026–32.

Gale EA. 1997. "Insulin Lispro: A New Quick-Acting Insulin Analogue." *Expert Opinion on Investigative Drugs* 6:1247–56.

Gastaldelli A, Ferrannini E, Miyazaki Y, Matsuda M, DeFronzo RA. 2004. "Beta-Cell Dysfunction and Glucose Intolerance: Results from the San Antonio Metabolism (SAM) Study." *Diabetologia* 47:31–39.

Goldberg B, Goldberg MA. 2002. *Alternative Medicine.* San Francisco: Celestial Arts.

Grady D. 2006. "Genetic Test for Diabetes May Gauge Risk, But Is the Risk Worth Knowing? *New York Times*, August 8.

Grundy SM, Benjamin IJ, Burke GL, Chait A, Eckel RH, Howard BV, Mitch W, Smith SC, Sowers JR. 1999. "Diabetes and Cardiovascular Disease: A Statement for Healthcare Professionals from the American Heart Association." *Circulation* 100:1134–46.

Haardt MJ, Selam JL, Slama G, Bethoux JP, Dorange C, Mace B, Ramaniche ML, Bruzzo F. 1994. "A Cost-Benefit Comparison of Intensive Diabetes Management with Implantable Pumps versus Multiple Subcutaneous Injections in Patients with Type I Diabetes." *Diabetes Care* 17:847–51.

Henriksen EJ. 2006. "Exercise Training and the Antioxidant Alpha-Lipoic Acid in the Treatment of Insulin Resistance and Type 2 Diabetes." *Free Radical Biology and Medicine* 40:3–12.

Henschen F. 1969. "On the Term Diabetes in the Works of Aretaeus and Galen." *Medical History* 13:190–92.

Hlebowicz J, Darwiche G, Björgell O, Almér LO. 2007. "Effect of Cinnamon on Postprandial Glucose, Gastric Emptying, and Satiety in Healthy Subjects." *American Journal of Clinical Nutrition* 85:1552–56.

Jovanovic L. 2007. "Screening and Diagnosis of Gestational Diabetes Mellitus." Available at: http://www.utdol.com/utd/content/topic.do?topicKey=pregcomp/28647&selected Title=1~2001&source=search_result.

Kahn CR, Weir GC. 1994. *Joslin's Diabetes Mellitus*. 13th ed. Philadelphia: Lea & Febiger.

Kahn R. 2007. "Type 1 Diabetes." Available at: http://www.dlife.com/dLife/do/ ShowContent/type1_information.

Karter AJ, Ahmed AT, Liu J, Moffet HH, Parker MM, Ferrara A, Selby JV. 2004. "Use of Thiazolidinediones and Risk of Heart Failure in People with Type 2 Diabetes: A Retrospective Cohort Study." *Diabetes Care* 27:850–51.

Kavic MS. 1997. *Laparoscopic Hernia Repair*. London: Informa Healthcare.

Kim D, MacConell L, Zhuang D, Kothare PA, Trautmann M, Fineman M, Taylor K. 2007. "Effects of Once-Weekly Dosing of a Long-Acting Release Formulation of Exenatide on Glucose Control and Body Weight in Subjects with Type 2 Diabetes." *Diabetes Care* 30:1487–93.

Kimmelstiel P, Wilson C. 1936. "Benign and Malignant Hypertension and Nephrosclerosis: A Clinical and Pathological Study." *American Journal of Pathology* 12:45–48.

King H, Aubert RE, Herman WH. 1998. "Global Burden of Diabetes, 1995–2025: Prevalence, Numerical Estimates, and Projections." *Diabetes Care* 21:1414–31.

Kinshuck D. 2007. "Cataracts in Diabetes." Available at: http://medweb.bham.ac.uk/ easdec/cataracts_in_diabetes.html.

Kleinfield NR. 2006. "Bad Blood: Diabetes and Its Awful Toll Quietly Emerge as a Crisis." *New York Times*, January 9.

Kulkarni KD. 2004. "Food, Culture, and Diabetes in the United States." *Clinical Diabetes* 22:190–92.

Landsberg L, Molitch M. 2004. "Diabetes and Hypertension: Pathogenesis, Prevention, and Treatment." *Clinical and Experimental Hypertension* 26:621–28.

Leichter S. 2001. "Assessing New Products in Diabetes: A Business Model in Support of Clinical Decision-Making." *Clinical Diabetes* 19:78–80.

Liburd LC. 2003. "Identity and African-American Women with Type 2 Diabetes: An Anthropological Perspective." *Diabetes Spectrum* 16:160–65.

Luderitz B. 2002. *History of the Disorders of Cardiac Rhythm*. Malden, MA: Blackwell Publishing.

Magner LN. 2005. *A History of Medicine*. 2nd ed. New York: Taylor & Francis Group.

Majeed A. 2005. "How Islam Changed Medicine." *British Medical Journal* 331:1486–87.

Markwick A. 1842. *An Essay on Diabetes*. London: A. Pigott.

Masharani U, Karam J, German M. 2004. "Pancreatic Hormones and Diabetes Mellitus." In Gardner DG, Greenspan FF, eds., *Basic and Clinical Endocrinology*, 658–746. New York: McGraw-Hill.

McCulloch DK. 2006. "Patient Information: Foot Care in Diabetes." Available at: http://patients.uptodate.com/topic.asp?file=diabete/4428.

McCulloch DK. 2007a. "Evaluation of the Diabetic Foot." Available at: http://www. utdol.com/utd/content/topic.do?topicKey=diabetes/10219&selectedTitle=3~25& source=search_result.

McCulloch DK. 2007b. "Glycemic Control in Type 2 Diabetes Mellitus: Persistent Hyperglycemia and Long-Term Therapy." Available at: http://www.utdol.com/utd/ content/topic.do?topicKey=diabetes/24304&view=print.

Medvei VC. 1993. *The History of Clinical Endocrinology*. Pearl River, NY: Parthenon.

Mendoza JA, Drewnowski A, Christakis DA. 2007. "Dietary Energy Density Is Associated with Obesity and the Metabolic Syndrome in U.S. Adults." *Diabetes Care* 30:974–79.

Morgan R. 2006. "How to Eat to Prevent or Treat Diabetes." News release, American Diabetes Association.

Mudalia S. 2007. "New Frontiers in the Management of Type 2 Diabetes." *Indian Journal of Medicine* 125:275–96.

Nathan DM. 2007. "No Time to Inhale: Arguments Against Inhaled Insulin in 2007." *Diabetes Care* 30:442–43.

National Diabetes Information Clearinghouse. 2006. "Diabetes Overview." Available at: http://diabetes.niddk.nih.gov/dm/pubs/overview.

National Eye Institute. 2006. "Cataract." Available at: http://www.nei.nih.gov/health/cataract/cataract_facts.asp.

National Institute of Diabetes and Digestive and Kidney Diseases. 2005. *National Diabetes Statistics Fact Sheet: General Information and National Estimates on Diabetes in the United States, 2005.* Bethesda, MD: U.S. Department of Health and Human Services, National Institutes of Health.

National Institute of Diabetes and Digestive and Kidney Diseases. N.d. "The Environmental Determinants of Diabetes in the Young (TEDDY) Consortium." Available at: http://www.niddk.nih.gov/patient/TEDDY/TEDDY.htm.

National Institutes of Health. 2001. "Stem Cells and Diabetes." Available at: http://stemcells.nih.gov/info/scireport/chapter7.asp.

National Institutes of Health. 2007. "Calculate Your Body Mass Index." Available at: http://www.nhlbisupport.com/bmi.

National Kidney and Urologic Diseases Information Clearinghouse. 2005. "Your Kidneys and How They Work." Available at: http://kidney.niddk.nih.gov/kudiseases/pubs/yourkidneys/#top.

National Library of Medicine. 2000. *Classics of Traditional Chinese Medicine.* Available at: http://www.nlm.nih.gov/hmd/chinese/emperors.html.

National Library of Medicine. 2007. *ClinicalTrials.gov.* Available at: http://clinicaltrials.gov/ct/gui/action/FindCondition?ui=D003920&recruiting=true.

Nordmann AJ, Nordmann A, Briel M, Keller U, Yancy WS, Brehm BJ, Bucher HC. 2006. "Effects of Low-Carbohydrate versus Low-Fat Diets on Weight Loss and Cardiovascular Risk Factors: A Meta-Analysis of Randomized Controlled Trials." *Archives of Internal Medicine* 166:285–93.

Omachi R. 1986. "The Pathogenesis and Prevention of Diabetic Nephropathy." *Western Journal of Medicine* 145:222–27.

Papaspyros NS. 2000. *The History of Diabetes Mellitus,* 2nd ed. Stuttgart: Georg Thieme Verlag.

Paustian T. 2000. "Anabolism." Available at: http://dwb.unl.edu/Teacher/NSF/C11/C11Links/www.bact.wisc.edu/microtextbook/metabolism/Anabolism.html.

Personal Health Zone. 2005. "What Is the Status of Diabetes Research?" Available at: http://www.personalhealthzone.com/disease/diabetes/diabetesresearch.html.

Pham PC, Pham PM, Pham SV, Miller JM, Pham PT. 2007. "Hypomagnesemia in Patients with Type 2 Diabetes." *Clinical Journal of the American Society of Nephrology,* published online, January 3. Available at: http://cjasn.asnjournals.org/cgi/content/full/2/2/366.

Philpott T. 2006. "I'm Hatin' It: How the Feds Make Bad-for-You Food Cheaper Than Healthful Fare." *Grist,* February 22. Available at: http://www.grist.org/news/maindish/2006/02/22/philpott.

Pho K. 2005. "Diabetes." Available at: http://www.nlm.nih.gov/medlineplus/ency/article/001214.htm.

Poretsky L. 2002. *Principles of Diabetes Mellitus.* New York: Springer.

Powers A. 2004. *Harrison's Principles of Internal Medicine.* 16th ed. New York: McGraw-Hill Professional.

Powers MA. 1996. *Handbook of Diabetes Medical Nutrition Therapy.* Boston: Jones and Bartlett.

Prioreschi P. 2001. *A History of Medicine.* Omaha, NE: Horatius Press.

Reece EA, Coustan DR, Gabbe SG, eds. 2004. *Diabetes Mellitus in Women: Adolescence Through Pregnancy and Menopause.* 3rd ed. Philadelphia: Lippincott Williams & Wilkins.

Riddle MC, Drucker DJ. 2006. "Emerging Therapies Mimicking the Effects of Amylin and Glucagon-Like Peptide." *Diabetes Care* 29:435–49.

Riste L, Khan F, Cruickshank F. 2001. "High Prevalence of Type 2 Diabetes in All Ethnic Groups, Including Europeans, in a British Inner City." *Diabetes Care* 24:1377–83.

Rodriguez B. 1999. "Apple-Shaped Profiles Linked to Insulin Resistance." Available at: http://record.wustl.edu/archive/1999/03-25-99/articles/insulin.html.

Rosalie DA. 2000. *The Experience of Ancient Egypt.* Oxford: Routledge.

Rosner F. 1997. *The Medical Legacy of Moses Mamonides.* Jersey City, NJ: KTAV Publishing House.

Samhita C, ed. 1949. *The Caraka Samhita.* Vol. 1. Jamnagar, India: Shree Gulabkunverba Ayurvedic Society.

Sanders LJ. 2001a. "From Thebes to Toronto and the 21st Century: An Incredible Journey." *Diabetes Spectrum* 15:56–60.

Sanders LJ. 2001b. *The Philatelic History of Diabetes: In Search of a Cure.* Alexandria, VA: American Diabetes Association.

Scheiner G. 2004. *Think Like a Pancreas.* Washington, DC: Marlowe & Company, 2004.

Schneider BE, Mun EC. 2005. "Surgical Management of Morbid Obesity." *Diabetes Care* 28:475–80.

Selam JL, Charles MA. 1990. "Devices for Insulin Administration." *Diabetes Care* 13:955–79.

Shereen Arent JD. 2003. "The Role of Health Care Professionals in Diabetes Discrimination Issues at Work and School." *Clinical Diabetes* 21:163–67.

Singer GM, Geohas J. 2006. "The Effect of Chromium Picolinate and Biotin Supplementation on Glycemic Control in Poorly Controlled Patients with Type 2 Diabetes Mellitus: A Placebo-Controlled, Double-Blinded, Randomized Trial." *Diabetes Technology and Therapeutics* 8:636–43.

St. Lukes Cataract and Laser Institute. 2007. "Diabetic Retinopathy." Available at: http://www.stlukeseye.com/Conditions/DiabeticRetinopathy.asp.

Strathern P. 2005. *A Brief History of Medicine: From Hippocrates to Gene Therapy.* New York: Carroll & Graf.

Swartout-Corbeil DM. 2002. "Diabetes Mellitus." In Krapp K, ed., *Encyclopedia of Nursing and Allied Health.* Farmington Hills, MI: Gale Group.

Tang J, Wingerchuk DM, Crum BA, Rubin DI, Demaerschalk BM. 2007. "Alpha-Lipoic Acid May Improve Symptomatic Diabetic Polyneuropathy." *Neurologist* 13:164–67.

Thompson SR. 2005. "Gestational Diabetes." Available at: http://www.nlm.nih.gov/ medlineplus/ency/article/000896.htm.

Tillotson AK. 2001. *The One Earth Herbal Sourcebook*. New York: Kensington Books.

Trief PM, Morin PC, Izquierdo R, Teresi JA, Eimicke JP, Goland R, Starren J, Shea S, Weinstock RS. 2006. "Depression and Glycemic Control in Elderly Ethnically Diverse Patients with Diabetes." *Diabetes Care* 29:830–35.

Triplitt C, Chiquette E. 2006. "Exenatide: From the Gila Monster to the Pharmacy." *Journal of the American Pharmaceutical Association* 46:44–52.

Tripp-Reimer T, Choi E, Kelley LS, Enslein JC. 2001. "Cultural Barriers to Care: Inverting the Problem." *Diabetes Spectrum* 14:13–22.

Unschuld PU. 1986. *Nan-Ching*. Berkeley: University of California Press.

Walford RL. 2000. *Beyond the 120-Year Diet*. New York: Thunder's Mouth Press.

Warshaw H. 1996. *Diabetes Meal Planning Made Easy*. Alexandria, VA: American Diabetes Association.

Watkins PJ. 2003. *ABC of Diabetes*. 5th ed. London: BMJ Publishing Group.

White JR, Campbell RK. 2001. "Inhaled Insulin: An Overview." *Clinical Diabetes* 19:13–16.

Wild S, Roglic G, Green A, Sicree R, King H. 2004. "Global Prevalence of Diabetes Estimates for the Year 2000 and Projections for 2030." *Diabetes Care* 27:1047–53.

Williams G, Pickup JC. 2004. *Handbook of Diabetes*. 3rd ed. Malden, MA: Blackwell Publishing.

Wilmore JH. 2004. *Physiology of Sport and Exercise*. New York: Human Kinetics.

Wilmore JH. 2004. *Physiology of Sport and Exercise*. New York: Human Kinetics.

Winckler W, Graham RR, de Bakker PIW, Sun M, Almgren P, Tuomi T, Gaudet D, Hudson TJ, Ardlie KG, Daly MJ, Hirschhorn JN, Groop L, Altshuler D. 2005. "Association Testing of Variants in the Hepatocyte Nuclear Factor 4α Gene with Risk of Type 2 Diabetes in 7,883 People." *Diabetes* 54:886–92.

Index

About the Author

ANDREW GALMER is a freelance writer who currently studies at the New York College of Osteopathic Medicine.